THE INVISIBLE POWER OF MONEY

The Invisible Power of Money.
Author: Jorge Zaguirre Villanueva.
Registration Number: 04 / 2024 / 4275.
Intellectual Property Object: Literary Work.

First Edition: September 2024.
Publication Platform: Amazon KDP.

ISBN: 9798300054649.

Legal Notice:

@elpoderinvisibledeldinero

@poderinvisibledeldinero

What We Are Never Told and What We Should All Know.

If you are expecting a book written by expert economists, this is not for you.

Jorge Zaguirre Villanueva

ACKNOWLEDGEMENTS

This book would not have been possible without the unconditional support of my partner, Silvia Viñas. From the first day we met, you have been by my side, supporting me at every moment and never leaving my side, even in the worst moments and despite all the difficulties we have experienced along the way. Thank you for teaching me to be more demanding of myself every day, for motivating me to overcome all challenges, no matter how invincible they may seem, and for being my greatest source of inspiration and strength.

Thanks to my sister, María Zaguirre, for being an essential part of every project in our lives, despite the sacrifices that this has entailed. Your permanent support, your dedication and the strong family relationship that we have built together since we were so young have been fundamental to achieve our goals. Thank you for always trusting me, you are an indispensable pillar in the construction of all our dreams.

To my parents, Antonio and María, I would like to express my deep gratitude for having chosen a path full of challenges and for having faced each of them with courage. Thank you for the entrepreneurial spirit that you awakened in us, your children, and for instilling in us the desire to be entrepreneurs and not to be satisfied with the situation of the environment in which we were born. Your example of self-improvement has been the driving force behind our lives and our ambitions.

To my grandparents, I thank you for teaching us what real difficulties in life mean. They showed us by example what humility and simplicity are, and taught us to be people of integrity at all times. Thank you for showing us that, even if you start from a very low point, life, as in any race, is not measured by how you start, but by how far you get.

I would also like to thank my mother-in-law, my father-in-law who accompanied us until his last day, and my sister-in-law, for all their trust and support. Since the beginning of all our projects, you have been there, trusting us and giving us the necessary support to move forward. Thank you for being an example of overcoming difficulties and for always reminding us that difficulties are just steps towards success.

And finally, thanks to all our family and friends such as Niklas Heinecker, Badir Almusharrekh, Susana Jorreto, Domingo Valdivia, Antonio Lorente, José Sanchez, Dolores Manzanares and my great brother-in-law Sam Holland who have trusted us and who are always present in our day-to-day work. Your support and unwavering faith have given us the necessary strength to make all our goals a reality.

My deepest thanks to each of you for all your unwavering support.

THE INVISIBLE POWER OF MONEY

INDEX

The two most important days of your life are the day you are born and the day you find out why.

"Mark Twain.

FOREWORD

My name is Jorge Zaguirre Villanueva. I began writing this book at the age of 36, an age at which many consider that there is still much to live, but the truth is that, in this time, I have accumulated experiences and lessons that have left a deep mark on me. Life, although it sometimes seems short, offers us countless opportunities to grow, adapt and rediscover ourselves.

I have lived long enough to understand that youth is not a matter of age, but of the ability to keep alive a curiosity, a passion for learning and a desire to contribute positively to the world. In an environment where change is rapid and relentless, I have learned that our true strength lies in adaptability and the determination to continue, even when the road becomes uncertain.

I was born in Almería, a city bathed by sun and sea, in southern Spain, and grew up in a humble family, in a neighbourhood where life was a constant challenge. I studied in a public school near a slum, surrounded by people who, like my family, struggled every day to get ahead. Despite our limitations, my parents always taught me to see the world from different perspectives, instilling in me the ability to understand the political and social differences that exist in our country. This education allowed me to develop a more balanced and empathetic view of life, able to respect and analyse opinions from all angles.

My life has been full of trials and learnings. In the past few years, I have faced three surgeries for cancer. The most recent occurred just a few months ago, and although I am now on constant medical surveillance to ensure that the disease does not return, each experience has left a deep mark on me.

The first operation was particularly difficult: a tumour measuring more than nine centimetres in the spinal canal left me paralysed from the waist down. In that instant, my world fell apart. Losing the ability to walk is something that cannot be described in words; it is an experience that transforms your perception of life and forces you to rethink everything. But, surprisingly, it also gave me a unique opportunity: to relearn how to walk, to feel again the thrill and effort of taking each step, to experience resilience in its purest form.

I grew up in a home where money was always scarce, but where love and support were never lacking. My grandfather was a central figure for our whole family, a person who lived his childhood in abject poverty, but who never stopped fighting for his family. He used to tell me firmly: "Son, there is nothing harder for a father than to tell his children that he has nothing to feed them". He and my grandmother taught us all the true meaning of survival, of what it means to live without resources, and the importance of resilience.

My grandfather worked day and night, first in his home village of Bacares, in the Sierra de Los Filabres, and then in Lyon and Paris, where he emigrated alone in search of a better future for his family. At night, he was a miner at the Las Menas mine; during the day, he worked in the fields, tending the animals and crops. He lived whole days with hardly any sleep, and when the fatigue was unbearable, he would tie himself to his donkey so as not to fall off in his sleep and move from one job to the next.

Eventually, he made the difficult decision to emigrate to France, where the salary as a labourer was five times higher than anything he could scrape together with two jobs in Spain. He spent more than ten years in France, sending every penny of his salary home to ensure that his wife and daughters could survive and improve their quality of life. His sacrifice was immense, and although he was sometimes unable to come home even once a year, he always remembered what he told them the day he left: "Don't shed a tear, they are not taking me prisoner, I am leaving to fight for the continuity of our lives".

Last year, my grandfather left us, the morning after Christmas Eve. Even in his final hours, he showed the strength that always characterised him in keeping the family together, staying with us through Christmas dinner, even though he could barely breathe. In the early hours of the morning, he departed, leaving us a legacy of hard work, perseverance and unconditional love.

I grew up under the influence of his example, working alongside him in the fields, picking almonds from the ten hectares that he himself planted with his own effort. We spent long days together, and even though he was over 70 years old, he still climbed an almond tree, beating with a stick until the last almond fell to the ground.

His perseverance and dedication left a deep impression on me, and it was then that I began to question what money really was. How could something so intangible have so much power over our lives?

I looked everywhere for answers, but none seemed to satisfy my curiosity. Not even when I studied business studies at university did I manage to find the clarity I was looking for. It was then when I finished my studies that I decided to embark on a path of self-education, immersing myself in dozens of readings and experiences that led me to write this book.

A book that seeks not only to understand what money is, but also how we can use it to build a fairer world, where resources are not hoarded by a few, but distributed fairly to improve the lives of all.

Throughout this journey, I have found inspiration in the teachings of great authors and entrepreneurs such as Robert Kiyosaki and the biographies of Elon Musk, Steve Jobs, Ray Kroc, Bill Gates or Mark Zuckerberg, whose ideas have been a guide in my life and that I hope can also guide you. Facing my illnesses has led me to understand that the two most important days of your life are indeed the day you are born and the day you discover why. Because when you face the possibility of never walking again or living much longer, you realise that the only thing that really matters is whether you have contributed enough before you leave to achieve the greatest possible satisfaction: the self-realisation of having helped others to create a better world.

This book is my attempt to contribute to that purpose in a deeper and more meaningful way. It is more than just a guide or a financial toolkit; it is an invitation to reflect on the true power of money and its impact on our lives and society. My hope is that every page will inspire you to not only improve your financial situation, but also to question and redefine your relationship with money. I want this book to empower you to take control of your life, so that you can make your money work for you and not the other way around.

But my greatest hope is that, through these words, you will discover or strengthen your purpose. Because at the end of the day, the most important thing is not how much money you have, but how you choose to use it to positively impact the lives of others. I want you to see money not just as a tool to meet material needs, but as a means to create real change, to improve the lives of those around you, and to build a legacy that transcends financially.

My hope is that, with this book, you will find the inspiration to align your finances with your values and, ultimately, with your life purpose. Because when we use money with intention and conscience, we not only transform our reality, but we also contribute to building a more just and equitable world for all.

CHAPTER 1

THE POWER OF MONEY: WHAT IS IT REALLY?

CHAPTER 1

THE POWER OF MONEY: WHAT IS IT REALLY?

From a very young age, I always had an insatiable curiosity about what money was. I knew that understanding it would be crucial to my survival when the day came that I would depend solely on myself to make it. I grew up in an era when we were constantly told: "Study hard and you will find a good job that will earn you a lot of money". But there was something about that statement that didn't quite convince me. I sensed that the reality was much more complex, that money was not just a reward for hard work.

Now, in the year 2024, if we look for a definition of what money is, we find the following descriptions in the RAE and Wikipedia:

RAE:

1. m. Current currency.
2. m. Treasury, fortune.
3. m. A silver and copper coin used in Castile in the 14th century and which was equivalent to two cornados.
4. m. Ancient silver coin of Peru.
5. m. penny (‖ British currency worth one hundredth of a pound sterling).
6. m. Ochavo (‖ coin).
7. m. Weight of 24 grains, equivalent to 11 g and 52 cg, which was used for silver coins and objects.
8. m. Econ. Generally accepted means of exchange or payment.

Wikipedia: Money is any asset or good generally accepted as a means of payment by economic agents for their exchanges and which also fulfils the functions of being a unit of account and a store of value. Examples of money are: coins, currencies and banknotes, debit cards and electronic transfers, among others.

These definitions, although technical and correct, leave a feeling of dissatisfaction. They seem to explain everything and nothing at the same time. Through these words, we fail to grasp the essence of money and the power it exerts in our lives. It is as if we were trying to define air by describing only its chemical composition, not to mention the vitality it gives us. In fact, over the years, I have found that many people, even those who appear to be financially successful, do not fully understand what money is either. Some authors suggest that this is not accidental, but a deliberate strategy on the part of those who control the world's wealth. It is said that an elite manipulates information, keeping the rest in ignorance in order to preserve their privileged position. I don't know if this is entirely true, but I wouldn't be surprised if it is.

What is clear to me is that the time has come for us to take off the blindfold and understand what money really is, so that we can fight for a world where resources are distributed more equitably.

The Origin of Money and its Evolution

To understand what money is, it is essential to know a key milestone in economic history: until 1971, countries printed coins based on the amount of gold they owned, a practice known as the gold standard. This system ensured that each banknote issued had a tangible gold backing. However, this all changed when, due to enormous economic pressures, especially arising from the First World War, governments began printing money without having sufficient gold reserves to back it up. The need to finance the war effort led to uncontrolled banknote issuance, which eventually led to a decoupling of money from its precious metal backing.

Throughout history, different cultures have used various goods as money: shells, cattle, salt, tobacco, metals, and of course, gold. Among all of them, gold stood out for its unique characteristics: it is durable, divisible, homogenous and difficult to counterfeit. These qualities made it the liquid good par excellence, accepted as a currency of exchange in almost every culture on the planet.

To better understand the role of money, let us go back to the beginning of economic exchanges: barter. This practice, which emerged in the Neolithic period around 10,000 years ago, marked the beginning of agricultural and pastoral societies.

During the Neolithic, the economy ceased to be predatory, as it had been in the Palaeolithic, when hunter-gatherer societies depended directly on the available natural resources. With the invention of agriculture and animal husbandry, the economy became productive. This generated a surplus of goods, which allowed some people to engage in the production of other products, such as pottery, which they could exchange for the agricultural surplus.

However, this barter system was not perfect. Imagine that a farmer wanted to exchange a cow for potatoes, eggs or lettuce. Not all producers of these goods needed beef at the time, which created a mismatch in the exchanges. Thus was born the need to establish a commonly accepted medium of exchange: money.

Early Coins and Trust Money

The move towards the first coins was a revolutionary change in human economic history. The first metal coins are believed to have been minted in Lydia, a region of Asia Minor, around the 7th century BC. These coins, made of an alloy of gold and silver called electro, were stamped with symbols indicating their weight and value. This greatly simplified trade, as people could now use these coins to buy goods and services without the need for direct agreement on the value of the goods.

With the minting of coins, trade became easier and more efficient. Coins had an agreed value and were easy to transport, allowing people to trade not only within their local communities, but also with people in distant regions. This encouraged the development of trade routes and, in time, the expansion of empires.

Although coins were a major breakthrough, the next great leap in the evolution of money was the invention of paper money. The use of paper money began in China during the Tang dynasty (618-907 AD), but it was under the Song dynasty (960-1279 AD) that paper money came into use on a large scale. Paper money was a response to the need for a more practical and lighter medium of exchange than heavy metal coins, especially in a country as vast as China.

Paper money, at first, represented a certificate that could be exchanged for metal coins deposited in government warehouses. Over time, however, people began to accept paper money at face value, without worrying about exchanging it for precious metals. This change marked the birth of what we know today as **fiat money**, i.e. money that has value because people trust it, not because it is backed by a tangible asset such as gold or silver.

The End of the Gold Standard and the Age of fiat money

The concept of fiat money, or trust-based money, continued to evolve and eventually replaced the gold standard. Until the early 20th century, most coins and banknotes issued by governments were backed by gold reserves. This meant that in theory, anyone could go to a central bank and exchange their money for an equivalent amount of gold.

However, during World War I, many countries suspended the gold standard in order to print more money to finance the war effort. This led to massive inflation in some countries, such as Germany, where hyperinflation became a devastating crisis. After World War II, with the creation of the Bretton Woods system, the US dollar was pegged to gold, while other currencies were pegged to the dollar. This system, although stable, did not last long.

In 1971, US President Richard Nixon announced the end of the gold standard, which meant that the dollar, and by extension all other currencies, would no longer be backed by gold. This marked the beginning of the era of modern fiat money, where the value of money depends entirely on the trust people have in the government that issues it until the current era.

The Digital Age and Cryptocurrencies

We are currently experiencing a new evolution of money with the emergence of cryptocurrencies. Bitcoin, created in 2009 by an individual or group of individuals under the pseudonym Satoshi Nakamoto, is the first and best known cryptocurrency. Unlike fiat money, cryptocurrencies are not controlled by any government or central entity. Instead, they are based on blockchain technology, which is a decentralised registry that ensures the security and transparency of transactions.

Cryptocurrencies represent a direct challenge to the traditional financial system. Their decentralised nature means that they cannot be manipulated by governments in the same way as fiat money. Furthermore, cryptocurrencies are global, meaning that they can be used anywhere in the world without the need for intermediaries, such as banks.

Although cryptocurrencies are still in their early stages and face many challenges, they could represent the future of money. We are at a turning point in economic history, where money is moving from physical to digital, and where trust is placed not in governments, but in technology.

Money is not just a medium of exchange; it is a reflection of the society in which we live. Throughout history, money has evolved to suit people's needs and values. From barter to cryptocurrencies, each form of money has played a crucial role in the development of civilisation.

However, it is important to remember that money, in whatever form, is not an end in itself, but a means to other ends. True wealth is not measured only in terms of money, but in the quality of life, security and opportunities we can create for ourselves and others.

Today, we find ourselves in an era where the concept of money is changing again. While governments print money, we are also seeing the emergence of new forms of money. Despite the messages of fear surrounding digital money, it could represent a healthier system of exchange, free from the political manipulations that have bankrupted many nations. The ability of governments to print money at will, with no real basis in the creation of new goods or services, has been a major cause of economic instability throughout history.

A healthy monetary system should be based on the actual production of goods and services. Imagine again a neolithic economy where commodities such as meat, eggs, potatoes and milk are exchanged. A healthy economic system would only produce money in direct proportion to the value of the goods in circulation and would increase that amount only when new goods are created.

The fundamental problem of our global economy can be understood with a simple example: let's imagine that we get together with friends to play Monopoly, but the owner of the game does not tell us all the rules and starts handing out tickets. We would all concentrate on grabbing as much money as possible, but how could we do that if we don't know all the rules of the game? This is exactly what happens in our real economy. Governments play the same game as the rest of us, but with two big advantages: they know some of the rules and they have control of the banking system, which allows them to print money whenever they need to, with the serious consequence for everyone. While politicians continue to undermine the economic stability of countries by financing their deficit economies, they persist in printing money without backing it up, sustained only by increasing indebtedness. This cycle perpetuates periods of hyperinflation that erode citizens' purchasing power, devastating their economic capacity and leaving nations trapped in a vicious cycle of inflation and unsustainable debt.

As we will see below, inflation can have both positive and negative effects. "Good" inflation occurs when price increases reflect real growth in the production of goods and services in a healthy economy. In contrast, "bad" inflation arises when prices rise artificially due to excessive issuance of money without a back-up in the increase of goods and services. The latter does not represent real growth, but rather a devaluation of the currency in circulation, which reduces its purchasing power, creating a situation where most Central Banks usually try to counteract it by raising interest rates to rebalance the economy. However, this strategy often leads to an even greater economic crisis, as it raises financing costs, chills consumption and investment, and triggers a deep recession.

Imagine you have a cake to share among a group of friends. If suddenly more friends join the party, you will have to cut the cake into smaller portions so that everyone can have a piece.

This is similar to "bad" inflation: when more money is printed without an increase in goods and services, the value of each note is reduced, as if you were dividing the same pie among more people. The pie does not grow, but the slices do get smaller.

On the other hand, if you have one cake and decide to bake another because there are more friends, the extra cake represents "good" inflation: there is more to go around because the economy has grown, and everyone can enjoy a slice of the new cake without anyone getting less.

All economies, whether microeconomic or macroeconomic, depend on the same equation: *Income - Expenditure*. And this equation can have two outcomes:

1. Income - Expenditure = Positive.
2. Income - Expenditure = Negative.

A good or bad economy differs simply in its performance. If the result is positive, it is a well-managed economy, where income exceeds expenditure. If the result is negative, it is a poorly managed economy, where expenditure exceeds income. It is as simple as that, although we could find ourselves in a specific moment of negative results due to investment in growth, let's treat it as a situation maintained perpetually over time. There is no need to complicate it with unnecessary terminology or convoluted definitions that make us feel that we are not smart enough to understand the financial system. It is perfectly normal that, if it is not properly explained to us, we do not know how the system works. Just as a baby needs to be held by the hand to teach it to take its first steps, we need clear guidance to understand the economy.

This book is intended to be that guide. Not only do I want to explain what money is, but I also want to help you understand how the global economic system works and how you can use that knowledge to improve your life. It is time we all knew the rules of the game so that we can play the game on a level playing field.

CHAPTER 2

IS MONEY THE ENEMY? BUSTING MYTHS

CHAPTER 2

IS MONEY THE ENEMY? BUSTING MYTHS

Let us think back to the initial moment of the creation of money, in the Neolithic era. Money emerged as a general medium of exchange for the different goods and services produced in a society. In other words, money represented the labour time that each individual devoted to the creation of a good. Therefore, we can say that money = labour time. If we accept this premise, can we then say that working is bad? Definitely not. The idea that work is inherently negative is a misconception that has unfortunately infiltrated the perception of money.

We often fantasise about living on an island paradise, surrounded by endless riches, without ever having to worry about working again. But if we think about it, do you really think that would make you happy? The reality is much more complex. We crave money when we don't have it, but once we achieve financial stability, we are confronted with a deeper truth: what have we come into this world to do? To be miserly misers who spend every morning counting how much money they hoard in their bank accounts? Or, on the contrary, did we come here to contribute, to leave a positive mark on the world?

I have met people with so much money that they could feed their next 60 generations without working, and I can assure you that they have not found happiness in it. In fact, many of these people live in a constant search for meaning, trying to fill a void that money cannot fill. For me, the greatest self-realisation there is in life is to have made a positive contribution to this world during our brief time in it. Helping others is noble work, and if work is money, then money cannot be bad.

Let me repeat it clearly: money is NOT BAD. I put it in capital letters because last night I had the opportunity to have an intense dinner conversation with a Bolivian acquaintance who has travelled halfway around the world, passing through areas with hardly any resources. During our conversation, I tried to understand why she perceived money as a bad thing, referring to it as a "necessary evil good". I was intrigued by his perspective, so I tried to explain to him that money itself is not evil. If money is work and work is contributing and helping others, then we must change our perception. It is not the existence of money that is bad, but something much deeper, which I will explain below.

Unfortunately, I did not have the opportunity to go deeper into our conversation. Even though I explained to him that I come from a very humble family, his mind was closed when he thought that I was only interested in making money. He perceived me as a "capitalist" who does not think about helping others, but only about enriching his own pocket. This is a common, and sadly erroneous, perception that many people have about those who seek to understand and manage money. I asked him how he intended to help others if not through work, effort and, yes, also money. It is unfortunate that we could not continue, but I remain hopeful that, with patience, we will come to understand each other and put the pieces of the puzzle together to achieve our common goal: helping others to have a more financially balanced life.

So why does money have such a bad reputation?

There are countless occasions when, in meetings with friends or new acquaintances, tension arises when money is discussed. And why? If Money = Work and Work = Helping, what happens? The answer is simple: IGNORANCE. This is not ignorance resulting from a lack of personal interest in learning about money, but organised ignorance, a system designed to keep the majority of the population in the dark. This game is rigged so that only a few, those who know all the rules, can play the game to their advantage. As you have surely heard, information is power, but only when it is possessed by you and no one else.

This misperception that money is bad is deeply rooted in our culture, and is perpetuated from generation to generation. From a young age, we hear phrases like "money corrupts" or "money doesn't bring happiness", and while there is partial truth in these statements, the real problem is the lack of financial education and misinformation that surrounds us. It is time to erase the old cliché that money is bad. That is not the reality. The correct phrase should be: **it is the lack of knowledge about money that is really bad**.

Think for a moment: how many years do we spend studying, for example, to obtain a university degree? Three years of pre-school education, six years of primary education, four years of compulsory secondary education, two years of baccalaureate and four years of university, 19 years of our lives spent in education. In total, 19 years of our lives spent in education. And in how many of those years do they teach us about money? **NONE**. Yet we still believe that we are training to earn money, even though we have no idea how it really works.

This is no accident. The education system is designed to train workers, not to create financially independent and educated individuals. The aim is to produce people who fit into the existing structure, who know how to follow orders and how to fulfil their role in the economy, but who do not question the system or try to change it. This lack of financial education is one of the reasons why so many people struggle with their personal finances and fail to achieve economic stability.

When I was in high school, I was lucky enough to meet a great person whom I will never forget: José Hidalgo. Thanks to him, I was able to continue my academic training. He taught me that the most important thing in life was not to pass a subject, but to pass all the subjects in life. He did what no one else would have done: he took the title of a subject away from an ignorant professor who tried to make me believe that his subject was the most important in the world. Thanks to his support, today I have the opportunity to help many more.

Academic subjects are important, but the problem is that the subject we should really know about, money, is never taught. This omission is deliberate, and is perpetuated by an education system designed to train submissive workers with no financial literacy and little motivation to innovate or create.

Monopoly and the Rules of the Game

Let's go back to the example of Monopoly. Why do we say that governments, which allow such an education system, play with two big advantages?

1. **They know all the rules of the game.**
2. **They have control of the banking system so they can print money whenever they need it.**

They know the rules of the game, but they do not explain them so that they can play with an advantage and not reveal the true situation of the monumental economic bankruptcy hidden in their financial statements. And why do they do this? For a very simple reason: their financial equation is negative and heading towards a bottomless pit. Their Income - Expenditure is very, very negative. But the worst thing is that they are destroying the monetary system because they are practising the worst possible monetary policy: covering expenses with continuous increases in debt and printing more and more money to cover the bills. This causes a constant devaluation of all our assets, because a sound economy should only print more money when there is a real increase in the amount of goods produced, i.e. when there is a real increase in GDP.

Imagine for a moment what your situation would be like if you did the same thing. In the equation Income - Expenses = Positive or Negative, the negative result would not matter because you could cover it with debt. And if it wasn't enough, you could print more money to pay off your debts. But in the end, someone has to pay the bill. Such irresponsibility only puts more money into circulation, devaluing our currency and, with it, the purchasing power of all of us. In fact, some studies indicate that this can result in an average loss of purchasing power of more than 5% per year.

Politics and the Hidden Financial Truth

No matter which political party you vote for, I have never fully trusted any of them, and for good reason: right, left or centre, have they ever taken real responsibility for explaining the financial situation to the citizens? **NO.** Why? Because they would lose voters. It is easier to create constituencies, making people believe that you are representing their interests, by launching populist messages depending on how many votes you can win.

- Some of them are in favour of the companies...
- Others, in favour of the workers...
- Some defend historical memory...
- Others take a stand against figures of the past...
- Some support the Church...
- Others defend the right to abortion...

It doesn't matter what position they take; they all count votes to secure a good seat.

This pattern of political behaviour shows us that, at heart, the real concern is not to improve the lives of citizens, but to maintain power. In the end, what really matters to these politicians is maintaining control and making sure that the system continues to function in a way that benefits them, not necessarily the people.

I think it is time to open our eyes and to tell what they do not tell us: the true reality in which we find ourselves. The problem is not the money itself, but the ignorance surrounding how it works and the manipulation we are subjected to by those who know all the rules of the game.

This chapter aims to demystify the idea that money is evil. It is not money that corrupts, but the lack of knowledge about its true role and function in our lives. Only when we understand how money really works can we use it effectively to improve our lives and the lives of others. It is time we all had access to the rules of the game so that we can play the game on an equal footing and build a fairer world.

CHAPTER 3:

DEBT VS. SAVINGS: THE GREAT FINANCIAL DEBATE

CHAPTER 3:

DEBT VS. SAVINGS: THE GREAT FINANCIAL DEBATE

Ever since I was a child, I always heard at home that debt was the cause of our financial problems, that it kept us trapped in a life of limitations and should therefore be avoided at all costs. "Don't get into debt, don't take out a mortgage; you will be a prisoner of debt all your life", I was told. These words echoed in my head as a constant warning, an unquestionable truth that defined how I should handle my finances. I grew up with the belief that debt was a bad thing, something to be avoided like a contagious disease.

But over time, I began to question this long-held belief. Debt, what is it really? It is money, no more and no less, and is it really bad? The answer is much more complex than it seems. Debt is not inherently bad, just as money is not inherently bad. What can be detrimental is not fully understanding how debt works and how it can be used as a powerful tool in our lives. Debt can be both good and bad; it all depends on how we manage it. The key is to understand that debt can be used in two fundamental ways: to generate liabilities or to generate assets.

Liabilities vs. Assets: The Crucial Difference

First, let's clarify what liabilities and assets are. A liability is any asset that takes money out of our pocket, while an asset is an asset that generates income and therefore puts money in our pocket. This difference is fundamental to understanding why debt, when used wisely, can be a powerful tool in building wealth.

Consider a common example: a car. Traditionally, a car is thought of as a liability because it requires constant expenses: maintenance, fuel, insurance, taxes, etc. However, if that car is used as part of a car rental business, then it becomes an asset, generating income that can exceed the associated costs. The same is true of a home. Many people believe that owning a house is synonymous with wealth, but if the house only generates expenses and not income, then it is a liability. On the other hand, if that house is rented out and the rental income covers all expenses and also generates a surplus, then it becomes an asset.

This concept is vital to understanding how debt can be used effectively. If you use debt to acquire liabilities, you will end up in a downward spiral of rising costs and debt, as is the case with the vast majority of current ill-fated political administrations in many countries. But if you use debt to acquire income-generating assets, you are building a solid foundation for your financial future.

Debt as a Financial Tool

When I discuss debt with friends and acquaintances, I like to ask them two questions: "Would you like to make €3,444,000,000 profit a year?" and "Would you be willing to take on a debt of €86,955,000,000? The answer to the first question is always a resounding yes, while the second question usually provokes an uncomfortable silence.

Nobody wants to have such a large debt. So I tell them: "That's called the INDITEX Group".

Inditex, the fashion giant, is a perfect example of how debt can be used strategically to generate huge profits. The problem lies in the lack of financial education we have been taught from an early age. We have been taught to fear debt, to avoid it at all costs, but the reality is that debt, when managed properly, can be a powerful tool that allows you to achieve significant financial success.

Wealth is not measured simply by the amount of money you have, but by the amount of income you can generate from those resources. People who believe they are wealthy just by accumulating money in the bank are mistaken. If they do not invest that money to generate more income, their wealth will quickly vanish. This is often what happens to lottery winners: they spend all their money on liabilities, instead of investing it in assets, and soon find themselves back in poverty.

True wealth is measured by the amount of assets you own that are capable of generating income year after year. And this is where debt can play a crucial role. If you are able to use debt to acquire assets that generate income, you will be building sustainable and growing wealth. The key is to see debt not as a burden, but as a lever that allows you to access opportunities that would otherwise be out of reach.

The Case of Two Brothers and an Inheritance

Let us imagine a simple example to illustrate this concept. Two brothers, John and Paul, receive an inheritance from their parents. The family property is sold, and after paying taxes, each receives €120,000. John decides to buy a €60,000 car, a €25,000 boat, a €15,000 motorbike, and to spend €10,000 on travel, €5,000 on clothes and €5,000 on gifts for his friends. At first glance, it seems that Juan is enjoying his inheritance, surrounded by luxuries and comforts. He is the kind of person that society at large would see as successful and prosperous.

Paul, on the other hand, decides to use his inheritance differently. He is not concerned about what others think of his lifestyle, nor does he feel the need to impress anyone. Instead of spending his inheritance on consumer goods, he decides to invest in assets that can generate long-term income. His first idea is to buy a property in the centre of his city, which is experiencing population growth due to the expansion of local industry. However, instead of buying a single property for €120,000, Pablo decides to buy six houses of €100,000 each, financing 80% of each purchase with a mortgage.

To do so, he obtains total financing of €480,000 over 30 years at an interest rate of 1%. With this strategy, Paul becomes the owner of six homes, each of which generates a monthly rental income of €500. After deducting the mortgage payments (€260 per month per property), he earns a net profit of €240 per property, which translates into a total monthly income of €1,440. This is more than double the income he would have earned on a single property without using debt.

Most importantly, Paul has secured a steady income of €17,280 per annum. Assuming that Paul is 50 years old and expects to live another 30 years, his total income will amount to €518,400, plus the value of the properties, which at the end of the mortgage term will be fully paid off and valued at €600,000 (without taking into account the effects of accumulated inflation). In total, Pablo will have accumulated €1,118,400, almost ten times the initial inheritance.

Meanwhile, John, who in the short term appeared to be the rich brother, will have spent all his money on goods that do not generate income, and his wealth will have disappeared. What at first appeared to be a waste justified by momentary happiness becomes a trap that consumes all available resources without generating a sustainable return.

This example, broadly speaking, illustrates how debt, well managed, can be a powerful tool for generating wealth. However, it is important to consider other key factors, such as provisioning and risk management, as well as more advanced strategic financial concepts that will be discussed throughout the book.

People often confuse saving with provisioning, but they are very different concepts. Savings alone do not generate wealth. In fact, in an inflationary environment, savings erode and lose purchasing power over time. Provisioning, on the other hand, involves setting aside a portion of your resources to cover potential losses or to take advantage of future investment opportunities.

The Importance of Provisioning and Risk Management

Whenever you make an investment decision, you should always consider two scenarios: a positive and a negative one. It is crucial to have the necessary resources to deal with the worst-case scenario. This is especially important when working with debt, as a miscalculation or a change in the current economic situation can lead to significant financial problems. It should not be forgotten that the road to financial success is not linear, and making mistakes is part of the process. We live in an education system that punishes mistakes, but the reality is that mistakes are learning opportunities.

Thomas Edison, for example, failed more than 1,000 times before creating the first light bulb. There is no such thing as a perfect investment; what matters is learning from each experience and moving forward with consistency and perseverance. This is a principle that applies to any kind of investment, whether in real estate, business or any other field.

The above example should not be taken as a literal guide to investing. Every market is different, and the key is to find opportunities in areas that you are passionate about and where you have a competitive advantage. Real estate investment is just one of many possible options. What is essential is to have an asset-building mindset, rather than simply accumulating liabilities.

Savings: A Silent Trap

Savings, as traditionally promoted, can be a trap. Money that is not invested, that is not put to work, loses value over time due to inflation and other economic factors. As I mentioned at the beginning, the amount of money that is printed each year without a real proportion to the goods produced only causes a continuous depreciation of the currency. Keeping money stagnant in a savings account is not a viable strategy to generate wealth in the long run.

A personal example to illustrate this point that I always remember: my grandfather bought a farmhouse 40 years ago with his savings, paying €1,200 (200,000 of the old pesetas). Today, that rural estate has an appraised value of €120,000. If my grandfather had kept that money in a savings account, he would probably not have a penny today, as inflation and bank fees would have eroded its value over the decades. This is a clear lesson that money only generates value when it is put into motion, when it is invested in assets that can generate income and that grow in value annually for this very reason.

Money that is held and not actively used is losing value every day. Inflation, fees and market changes erode its purchasing power. This is why it is essential to change our mindset towards savings. Instead of seeing it as an end in itself, we should see it as a means to a greater goal: wealth creation through investment in productive assets.

The lesson here is clear: money only generates value when it is put into motion, when it is invested in assets that generate income. Saving alone is not enough to build sustainable wealth. We need to change our mindset and start seeing debt and investment as tools that, when used well, can transform our financial lives. Debt is not the enemy, but a powerful tool that, when used correctly, can be the key to building a life of abundance and financial security.

It is time to let go of unfounded fears about debt and start seeing it for what it really is: an opportunity to invest in our future, to build assets that generate income and to ensure that our wealth not only stays the same, but grows sustainably over time.

In short, debt is not bad; what is bad is not knowing how to use it. Savings, on the other hand, can be a trap if not used wisely. The key is to understand the difference between liabilities and assets, to learn how to manage risk, and to be willing to invest in ourselves and our future. Only then can we build a truly rich life, not just in financial terms, but in terms of freedom, security and personal satisfaction.

CHAPTER 4:

CONSUMERISM: THE 21ST CENTURY TRAP

CHAPTER 4:

CONSUMERISM: THE 21ST CENTURY TRAP

When we hear the phrase "consumerism is bad", it is easy for our minds to conjure up stereotypical images: factories in developing countries where workers are exploited, producing goods at low cost to satisfy the insatiable demand of Western markets. We see the wealthy entrepreneur, enjoying his life of luxury while thousands of workers suffer long hours for miserable wages. This is the narrative that has been inculcated into us to explain the inequalities of the modern world. However, as I often say, we often do not fully understand a problem because we do not spend enough time on it to understand its complexity.

It is easy to fall into the clichés that society repeats over and over again, without stopping to question whether we are really speaking with full knowledge of the facts. So rather than just accepting this simplistic view of consumerism, we need to dig deeper and try to understand what it really means and how it affects our lives in ways we may not have considered.

The Global Consumer Context

Consumerism, like any other economic phenomenon, cannot be analysed in absolute terms of good or bad. The problem lies not in the existence of consumption itself, but in how we manage it, how it affects our decisions and thus our lives. We often associate consumerism with labour exploitation in developing countries, but we must remember that exploitation can happen anywhere, whether it is in a factory in Bangladesh or an office in New York. Exploitation is a problem of working conditions, of lack of rights and protection, not necessarily of geography.

Moreover, it is important to understand that a person earning €500 per month in a country with a low cost of living may have a similar or even higher quality of life than someone earning €2,000 in a country where costs are much higher. What really determines the fairness of a wage is the purchasing power it provides, i.e. the amount of goods and services that can be purchased with that wage. This is a fundamental truth that is often overlooked in discussions about economics and social justice.

As we have discussed above, markets are governed by the law of supply and demand, and the world economy is nothing more than a vast set of "Monopolies" in which each country competes with its own currency. The value of these currencies (and the purchasing power they confer) depends on how many people are interested in acquiring that currency to buy the goods produced in that economy. Developing countries often have a competitive advantage in their early stages of growth: they can produce goods for the rest of the world at a lower cost, as their currency is not as strong in the global market, allowing them to sell products at very competitive prices abroad.

The Lesson of a 4-Year-Old Girl

A year ago, I had a revealing conversation with Martina, the four-year-old daughter of a friend. Although she was just a child, Martina showed an astonishing ability to grasp economic concepts that many adults still struggle to understand. Sitting at her kitchen table, her father and I started asking her questions about how she planned to earn money in the future: we asked her what she would sell, how she would do it, and where.

To our surprise, Martina confidently responded that she would set up a supermarket where she would sell bread and beer because she knew those products sold well. Moreover, she was clear that she would always keep large shelves full so that nothing would ever be out of stock. However, what truly amazed us was her response when we asked if she would need to buy the bread and beer at a lower price to make a profit. With all the naturalness in the world, Martina looked at us and asked, "Where do I buy it?"

In that moment, we realized that this four-year-old girl had understood in just a few years a lesson that takes many of us decades to learn: the key to success in any business lies in understanding and leveraging your competitive advantage. This is a perfect example of how consumerism, in its essence, is not inherently negative. The problem does not lie in the act of consuming but in not developing our innate ability to understand how we can create wealth and prosperity.

We all possess this capacity, yet we often lack the guidance to learn how to do it without harming others. The real question is not about consumption but about knowing how to manage and seize opportunities in a way that benefits both ourselves and our community. Little Martina taught us a great truth: if we know how to use our advantage, we can generate wealth without making others' lives worse.

Competitive Advantage in the Global Economy

The intelligence or ability to gain a competitive advantage does not depend on age or experience, but on a genuine interest in achieving an objective. In Spain, for example, it has been repeated for years that "the Italians steal our olive oil to sell it at higher prices, saying that it is theirs". However, the question that arises is: why have we not been the ones who have taken advantage of the opportunity to market our own product before to also obtain the added value that marketing provides?

Globalisation, often demonised, offers us the possibility of accessing global markets, allowing us not only to offer our products without geographical boundaries, but also to access goods and services produced in other parts of the world. The global free market is not an enemy; it is an opportunity to improve our lives and our economies. I myself have been intervened twice by tumours, using technology that was probably not developed in Spain. Thanks to that free market, I am still alive. Economies that choose to close themselves off to the outside world, that choose to rely only on the resources they produce themselves, are doomed to mediocrity. They will not be able to compete in a world where innovation and global collaboration are key to progress.

Economic Justice and Purchasing Power

The fairness or unfairness of a wage depends not only on its nominal amount, but also on the cost of living in each country. To illustrate this point, consider the difference between the most expensive loaf of bread in the world and the cheapest. In Singapore, one of the most expensive cities in the world, a 500-gram loaf of bread costs €2.1, while in Damascus, one of the cheapest cities, it costs €0.30. This means that a person earning €500 in Damascus can have similar purchasing power to someone earning €3,500 in Singapore. Ultimately, what matters is the relationship between the price of goods needed to live and the amount of income received.

For emerging economies, the biggest challenge is to access goods from abroad if they have not started to use their competitive advantage to export products at competitive prices. However, once they start to act astutely, we see once-poor economies become rich, while once-rich economies start to become poorer. This change is inevitable in a world where wealth does not disappear, but simply changes hands, just as energy is not destroyed, but changes state.

During a trip to Istanbul and Doha, I had the opportunity to learn about global economics in a way I never imagined. I observed how the prices of goods and services varied in a way that made no sense to me at first. In one country, restaurants were cheap, shops expensive and petrol expensive; in another, restaurants were expensive, shops normal and petrol cheap. What I discovered was that what a country is able to produce locally is sold at lower prices, while imported goods are almost uniformly priced around the world.

The Balance of Trade: The Engine of National Wealth

This is where the balance of imports and exports comes into play, which is primarily responsible for making a country rich or poor. Countries that possess goods demanded by the world market in large quantities have the advantage of capturing foreign currencies, enriching themselves in the process. Conversely, countries that rely heavily on imports and do not export enough to compensate for these expenditures see their wealth leak away to other countries. When we hear that our economy is going into recession, what it really means is that much of the money we emitted has gone into the wealth of other countries, because we have not been able to produce and sell more goods than we have bought.

So, is consumerism really bad? Is it bad to have needs? Is it bad to need to be fed, clothed, housed or educated? Is it bad to want to improve our quality of life day by day? Consumerism in itself is not bad. What can be harmful is unbridled consumerism, the irrational and excessive consumption that leads us to accumulate liabilities instead of investing in assets that provide us with long-term stability and growth.

The real problem with consumerism is not the need to consume, but the way we consume. Consumption that only satisfies immediate desires traps us in a cycle of dissatisfaction and economic dependence. However, conscious consumption, focused on investments that bring long-term security and well-being, can be a positive force for progress.

Furthermore, our responsibility lies not only in what we consume, but also in how it affects the planet. We must adopt a sustainable approach, choosing products and services that minimise environmental impact. This includes supporting the use of renewable energy, which is key to reducing our carbon footprint.

Today, renewable energy accounts for approximately 29% of global electricity production. However, generation capacity is much higher. With advanced technologies and appropriate policies, we could significantly increase this share, potentially reaching 80% or more in the coming decades. By promoting the use of solar, wind, hydropower and other clean sources, we not only contribute to sustainability, but also ensure a safer and healthier future for generations to come.

Equally important is our ability to reduce waste generation. The adoption of renewable and organic packaging, which decomposes without polluting, is a crucial step in this direction. Such packaging not only reduces environmental impact, but also fosters a circular economy, where materials are reused and recycled, thus minimising the need for new raw materials and reducing the burden on our planet.

Consuming responsibly, reducing waste and harnessing our capacity to generate renewable energy are not just options, but imperatives if we want a liveable planet and a stable economy in the long term.

Consumerism, like any other economic phenomenon, is multi-faceted. It is neither inherently bad nor good; it depends on how we manage it in our lives. What really matters is the awareness with which we consume, the ability to differentiate between what is necessary and what is superfluous, and the ability to invest in assets that provide us with long-term security and well-being.

In the end, the goal is not to demonise consumption, but to learn to consume wisely, so that our choices today build a stronger and more prosperous future for ourselves and for society at large, present and future. Misunderstood consumerism can lead to ruin, but when approached with knowledge and strategy, it can be a powerful tool for building the life we really want.

CHAPTER 5

THE PSYCHOLOGY OF MONEY AND FINANCIAL DECISION-MAKING

CHAPTER 5

THE PSYCHOLOGY OF MONEY AND FINANCIAL DECISION-MAKING

Money, beyond being a simple medium of exchange, has a profound psychological power that shapes our lives, decisions and overall well-being. How we think and feel about money directly influences how we manage it, invest it, spend it, and ultimately our ability to accumulate wealth or face financial difficulties. This chapter explores the intersection between psychology and finance, and how a deeper understanding of this relationship can help us make smarter and more sustainable financial decisions.

1. Financial Beliefs and Myths

From an early age, most of us develop beliefs about money based on what we learn from our parents, society and our own experiences. These beliefs can be either limiting or empowering, depending on their nature. For example, if you grew up in a home where it was said that "money is the root of all evil", you are likely to unconsciously associate wealth with something negative, which could lead you to sabotage your own opportunities for financial success.

Financial myths, such as the belief that only the wealthy can invest successfully, can also prevent us from making positive financial decisions. Dismantling these beliefs and myths is crucial to developing a healthier relationship with money. It is important to recognise that money itself is neither good nor bad; it is simply a tool that, when used wisely, can improve our lives and the lives of those around us.

2. The Power of Mindset: Abundance vs. Scarcity

The mindset with which you approach money has a profound impact on your financial results. People with an abundance mindset believe that there are enough resources and opportunities for everyone, and that their success does not come at the expense of others. This positive approach encourages creativity, investment in the future and a willingness to take calculated risks.

On the other hand, a scarcity mentality is characterised by the fear of losing what one has and the belief that resources are limited. This mentality can lead to conservative financial decisions, avoiding risks that could lead to growth. People with a scarcity mindset often focus on saving and protecting what they have rather than looking for opportunities to expand their wealth.

Adopting an abundance mindset does not mean ignoring risks or being reckless with money. Rather, it means recognising that the world is full of possibilities and that, with the right mindset and strategies, it is possible to create and sustain wealth over the long term.

3. Emotions and Money: The Impact of Fear and Euphoria

Money, like many other areas of our lives, is deeply connected to our emotions. Feelings such as fear, greed, euphoria and anxiety can cloud our judgement and lead us to make financial decisions that are not in our best long-term interest.

Fear is one of the most powerful factors influencing our financial decisions. It can manifest itself in many forms, such as fear of losing money, fear of making the wrong decisions or fear of financial uncertainty. This fear often leads to financial paralysis, where we avoid making important decisions or hold on to safe but underperforming investments.

On the other hand, euphoria, especially in rising markets, can lead to rash and irrational decisions. When markets are rising and everyone seems to be making money, it is easy to get carried away by the collective enthusiasm and take unnecessary risks. However, this type of behaviour often ends in losses when markets inevitably correct.

Understanding how our emotions influence our financial decisions is crucial to developing a sound financial strategy. By learning to control our emotions and maintain a balanced perspective, we can make more rational and effective decisions, even in times of volatility.

4. Developing a Healthy Financial Mindset

Once we understand the beliefs, mindset and emotions that influence our financial decisions, we can begin to develop a healthier financial mindset. This process begins with self-reflection and a willingness to question our existing beliefs and patterns of behaviour.

It is important to adopt habits that foster a positive relationship with money. This includes the regular practice of financial education, which enables us to make informed and strategic decisions. It is also crucial to set clear and realistic financial goals, which motivate us to keep going even in challenging times.

Another essential part of a healthy financial mindset is resilience. Throughout our financial lives, we are likely to face failures and setbacks. Rather than viewing these moments as definitive failures, it is important to see them as learning opportunities that strengthen us and set us up for future success.

5. Informed Financial Decision Making

The key to making smart financial decisions is information. As we are faced with various investment, spending and savings options, we must base our decisions on sound data and careful analysis rather than on emotions or unfounded beliefs.

Before making any major investment or financial commitment, it is crucial to do your homework. This includes researching the available options, understanding the risks involved and considering how each decision aligns with our long-term financial goals. It is also important to consult financial experts when necessary, especially in complex areas such as retirement planning or investing in volatile markets.

In addition, it is essential to recognise that financial decision-making is an ongoing process. Economic circumstances change, as do our personal needs and goals. Therefore, it is important to regularly review and adjust our financial strategies to ensure that we remain on the right track.

6. The Role of Financial Education

Financial education is the foundation on which a successful financial life is built. Without a solid understanding of how money, markets and the economy work, it is easy to fall into financial traps or make decisions that can ultimately be detrimental.

Unfortunately, formal financial education is lacking in many parts of the world. For this reason, it is vital that individuals take responsibility for educating themselves. This may involve reading financial books, participating in courses and seminars, or even seeking out financial mentors who can offer practical guidance and advice.

A good financial education not only helps you avoid costly mistakes, but also empowers you to take advantage of opportunities that others might overlook. By understanding the fundamentals of money and investing, you can make bolder, more strategic decisions that move you closer to your financial goals.

7. The Importance of a Healthy Relationship with Money

Ultimately, the psychology of money comes down to our relationship with it. By developing an abundance mindset, controlling our emotions, making informed decisions and engaging in ongoing financial education, we can build a healthier and more productive relationship with money.

This approach not only helps us achieve our financial goals, but also improves our overall quality of life. By seeing money as a tool that can be used to create opportunities and improve our lives, rather than an end in itself, we can achieve a greater sense of purpose and satisfaction in our financial and personal lives.

CHAPTER 6

COMPANIES AND WORKERS: DEBUNKING STEREOTYPES

CHAPTER 6

COMPANIES AND WORKERS: DEBUNKING STEREOTYPES

From the time I was a child, I was brought up with the idea that companies were evil, ruthless, predatory entities that only sought to take advantage of people. I was taught to see them as machines that squeeze workers, stealing their time and energy in exchange for miserable wages. In this narrative, the workers were always the heroes, the noble and helpless victims fighting against the tyranny of the bosses. This simplistic view took root in my mind for years, but over time, and especially after having worked for more than 15 years for two of Spain's leading multinationals, this perspective began to crumble.

In my experience, I became responsible for almost 400 workers, which allowed me to see the world from a much broader perspective. I interacted with managers, workers' legal representatives, civil servants, politicians, and workers themselves at all levels. It was then that I realised that this dichotomous view of "bad companies and good workers" is at best a dangerous simplification and at worst a lie that distorts reality.

The Real Division: Good and Bad People

What I discovered is that the real division is not between companies and workers, but between good people and bad people. No matter what title they bear - whether entrepreneur, director, legal representative, politician, civil servant or worker - what really matters is whether they are good or bad people. In each of these groups, I have met people with a deep sense of ethics and social responsibility, as well as others who acted purely out of self-interest, without caring about the consequences of their actions for others.

It is easy to fall into the trap of seeing entrepreneurs as the villains of the story. We imagine a wealthy person enjoying a life of luxury doing nothing more than reaping the fruits of other people's labour. However, this vision is both limited and wrong. Setting up a business, developing an idea, leading a project - all this requires considerable effort, hard work that is often not visible to the general public. An entrepreneur is also a worker, someone who devotes his or her time, energy and, in many cases, personal resources to turning an idea into a tangible reality. As in any other sphere of life, there are good and bad entrepreneurs, just as there are good and bad workers.

The Noise of the Bad and the Silence of the Good

One of the greatest tragedies of our society is that the voices of the good are often drowned out by the noise of the bad. At all levels, from corporate management to politics, there are people who act unethically, driven by greed and the desire for power. However, there are also many good people, who, out of fear, apathy or simple resignation, remain silent. This silence allows the bad guys to dominate the narrative, reinforcing stereotypes and perpetuating injustices.

It is crucial that all of us, regardless of our position, stop to reflect on the consequences of our actions. Shareholders and business owners must question whether there is a fair balance in the distribution of profits. My grandfather's saying is still relevant: without workers, there would be no companies, but without companies there would be no workers either. It is not acceptable to seek to maximise profits without considering ethics in the process. Social responsibility is not just a buzzword; it is an urgent necessity in a world where inequalities are increasing at an alarming rate.

Business managers must ensure that their decisions are not only profitable, but also ethically sound. They must align themselves with the values not only of the company, but also of the society in which they operate. Business ethics is not an optional luxury; it is a moral obligation that should guide all decisions.

Social Responsibility: Everyone's Commitment

Social responsibility does not only lie with entrepreneurs and managers. Civil servants, who manage resources that belong to everyone, cannot act carelessly simply because they have a secure position. Politicians, for their part, cannot make decisions that compromise the economic future of the country just to win votes or maintain their position of power. And workers cannot act as if their actions have no consequences for the company. The truth is that we are all interdependent as I said: without workers, there would be no enterprises, but without enterprises, there would be no workers either.

This is the time to realise that we live in a society where we must all take social responsibility. We cannot afford to act selfishly or irresponsibly, because our actions have an impact on the lives of others. We need a collective approach, where each of us does our bit to build a fairer and more balanced world.

During my years of experience, I have seen everything from managers obsessed with profitability, to workers abusing the system with fraudulent sick leave, harming not only the company, but also the rest of society. Abuse of the welfare system, such as high rates of absenteeism, is one of the reasons why our public coffers are in deficit, our competitiveness is in question and our productivity levels are at rock bottom. This misuse of public resources jeopardises essential services such as health, education and pensions, affecting the economic viability of our entire system, directly or indirectly.

Sustainable and Ethical Economy: A Moral Imperative

For a society to thrive, it is essential that its economy be sustainable, that income and expenses are balanced, and that ethical principles are applied in the distribution of resources. We often talk about the importance of ensuring economic support for those who arrive in our country under difficult circumstances. However, how can we effectively provide this help if our own finances are in crisis? It's like handing out fish without having enough fishing rods. If we allocate funds to aid that cannot be sustained due to a lack of jobs, we are building an unsustainable structure.

My grandfather, who emigrated to France 60 years ago, taught me a valuable lesson. He used to say, "Son, I almost didn't pass the medical tests for the job because my eyesight wasn't great for the position they offered me." What he really needed, and what he received, was a job, and thanks to that, he was able to contribute to society by building homes and earning a decent wage to support his family. This example reminds us that the key lies in providing real opportunities, not just temporary aid, so that people can thrive and help build a fairer society.

If we genuinely want to promote inclusion and the well-being of all, we must first create the necessary job opportunities. When unemployment rates are already high, how can we consider welcoming more people without first ensuring support for those already living here? It's not about closing doors but about opening them in a responsible and sustainable way.

As a country, we have both the capacity and responsibility to build an economy that facilitates the integration of those who wish to contribute and work with dignity. Additionally, it is crucial to simplify bureaucratic processes that make it difficult for newcomers to obtain legal status when they come here with the desire to build a future. Once regularization is facilitated, many will be able to make a living and contribute, integrating in a dignified manner into the labor force.

This is a matter of social responsibility: we must ensure that those who come find a viable path to integrate and prosper, avoiding false expectations that could lead them into difficult situations. With an inclusive and sustainable economy, we can not only help those who are already part of our society but also those who arrive seeking a better life.

Time for Urgent Change

The time has come to awaken the true intelligence that resides in each of us. We cannot continue to go with the flow, without worrying about whether at the end of the road there will be enough grass for everyone. We must stop and change many of the bad practices we have followed so far, without even asking ourselves whether we are destroying the environment in which we live. We need social responsibility, environmental responsibility and the awareness that each of us is responsible for the actions we take every day.

Change cannot wait. If we continue to procrastinate, we will be faced with the harsh reality that time has run out and it is too late to do anything. As someone once said to me: "If you want to change the world, start by changing yourself.

People who do not strive to contribute with their work to the creation of a better world, their time is running out. Those who greedily line their pockets with money, without concern for giving back fairly to society what society has given them, especially those who generate millions by running public services while maintaining miserable salaries, their time is running out. Politicians who focus only on their own profit, without concern for the common good, their time is also running out.

The Future: The Information Age and Responsibility

We are entering a new era, an information era that will mark a turning point in the intellectual evolution of human beings. We will be more and more people who, through the transmission of knowledge, will help others to understand the real keys to the financial strategies necessary to achieve a decent quality of life. This era will not be led by those who seek only their own profit, but by those who understand that true success is measured by the positive impact we have on society.

This is the moment of truth. A time for all of us, regardless of our position or role in society, to take responsibility for our actions and commit ourselves to building a fairer, more ethical and more sustainable future. It is not just about changing companies or workers, it is about changing everyone's mindset, about understanding that we are all in this together, and that only through collaboration, mutual respect and shared responsibility can we achieve a better world.

Social and Environmental Commitment: Integrating Success with Responsibility

In today's business world, success is not only measured by financial returns, but also by the impact we have on society and the environment. The strategies that distinguish great companies are those that not only seek profitability, but also pursue a greater purpose. In this sense, I would like to share a key aspect of my life that is aligned with this philosophy: my commitment to sustainability and social responsibility.

This commitment, among others, materialises with my participation as co-founder of Swappito (www.swappito.com), a platform that focuses on the reuse and exchange of goods between people, thus promoting a more responsible and sustainable consumption. Swappito not only addresses the problem of waste, but also creates a network of economic opportunities for those who participate in this collaborative model.

Like the successful strategies of large companies, Swappito takes an innovative approach to solving contemporary problems, demonstrating that it is possible to combine profitability with responsibility. In a world where excessive consumerism is having a significant environmental impact due to its lack of sustainability, our platform represents the future of conscious businesses, those that understand that true success includes creating a positive impact on the community and the planet.

I invite you to reflect on how you can integrate these principles into your own business strategies and decisions. By joining initiatives like Swappito, you will not only be growing your business in a sustainable way, but you will also be contributing to a global movement that seeks a balance between economic success and social responsibility.

Beyond Duality

In the end, companies are not inherently bad, nor are workers inherently good. Both are necessary for the functioning of society, and both have the potential to be forces for good or evil, depending on the choices made by the people involved. What really matters is ethics, responsibility and a willingness to do the right thing, not just for oneself, but for everyone.

The key to moving forward is to recognise our interdependence and work together to build a society where we can all prosper. It is time to leave simplifications behind and face the complexity of reality, each taking our share of responsibility for building a better world.

CHAPTER 7

GLOBALISATION: THREAT OR OPPORTUNITY?

CHAPTER 7

GLOBALISATION: THREAT OR OPPORTUNITY?

In our everyday conversations, globalisation is often mentioned with a tone of suspicion and rejection, almost always singled out as the main cause of the economic hardships faced by the majority of the population. There is a widespread perception that globalisation is a phenomenon that enriches the few at the expense of the many, and that the desire to better oneself in a globalised world is synonymous with greed and evil. But this is a limited and simplistic view. Globalisation, properly understood, is nothing more than the ability to share human creations, advances and knowledge on a global scale. And this ability has saved countless lives, including my own.

In 2016, a first tumour threatened to dry up my spinal cord. Three years later, in 2019, a second tumour was ready to spread and colonise my body. And in 2022, a third tumour tried again, repeating the same story. Each time, it was medical intervention, using technologies and knowledge developed in different parts of the world, that allowed me to survive. Had it not been for these advances, products of international collaboration and the global spread of knowledge, I would probably not be here to tell the story. That is why every day I give thanks to the medical professionals who were trained in this global knowledge and to globalisation itself, which made it possible for such advances to come into my life. Blessed globalisation, thanks to which I am still alive.

The Myth of Closed Economies

Throughout history, many countries have made the mistake of closing their economies, believing that this will protect their wealth from external "theft". This idea, while understandable from an emotional point of view, is deeply misguided and limits the possibilities for growth and prosperity. A closed economy is like a plant in a greenhouse without ventilation; at first it may appear strong, but over time it weakens and withers due to lack of exchange with the outside world.

Fear of the unknown, like fear of machines stealing our jobs, is a barrier that keeps us from moving forward. Technological and economic evolution is not an obstacle, but an opportunity to make our lives easier and more productive. Machines, far from taking jobs, free us from repetitive physical tasks, allowing us to focus our time and energy on mental work, where we can really generate added value.

Globalisation is, in essence, a catalyst for healthy competition. It drives us to offer better goods and services, to develop more advanced technology, to create medicines and solutions that improve the lives of people around the world. We fear globalisation because it forces us out of our comfort zone, to compete and to innovate. However, if we understand its benefits, we realise that fearing globalisation is like wanting to remain in the dark while others enjoy the light.

The Reality of Crises

Money, like energy, neither disappears nor is destroyed; it simply changes hands. When we speak of "crises", we refer to periods of change and redistribution, in which those who have failed to adapt or seize opportunities are disadvantaged. Crises, therefore, are not the direct result of globalisation, but of the inability of certain actors to adapt to a constantly changing environment.

Imagine a game of Monopoly, where each country has its own board and its own currency. Those countries that play most skilfully, creating goods and services demanded by others, reap the greatest rewards. These countries not only retain their wealth, but also attract money from other, less competent players, keeping their economies strong and balanced. It is a basic lesson of economics: those who work and prepare for the future reap the rewards of their efforts, while those who rest on their laurels are left behind.

This dynamic is similar to the story of the ant and the cicada: while the ant works diligently to gather resources, the cicada enjoys itself without worrying about tomorrow. When winter comes, the cicada finds itself with nothing, while the ant, thanks to its foresight and effort, is prepared to face adversity.

The Challenges of Developing Economies

One of the biggest challenges facing developing economies is the weakness of their currencies in the global market. A weak currency means that the country has limited purchasing power, making it difficult to acquire advanced technologies and restricting its ability to compete with global powers. While it may seem that these countries have the advantage of low labour costs, the real competitive advantage in the global economy lies in the productivity and quality of the products and services offered.

A country that continues to use traditional methods and does not invest in modern technology will be at a disadvantage. Globalisation offers the opportunity to access technologies and knowledge that can transform a country's economy, but to take advantage of these opportunities, the country in question needs to have an economy robust enough to participate in global exchange.

Economic Independence: Myth or Reality?

The idea of financial independence is attractive, especially in a world where self-sufficiency is associated with strength and autonomy. We all yearn for financial independence, but it is not achieved by isolating ourselves from the rest of the world. A truly independent economy is one that can generate its own resources and compete in the global marketplace. It is not about closing the doors to the outside world, but about opening them to take advantage of the opportunities offered by globalisation.

No sane parent would want their able and healthy child to stay at home all his or her life, unmotivated and purposeless. Similarly, countries that choose to isolate themselves from the world, that reject globalisation, condemn themselves to mediocrity and stagnation. Independence is not achieved by rejecting global collaboration, but by embracing it and using its benefits to strengthen the domestic economy.

Economic Nationalism and its Consequences

In recent years, we have seen a resurgence of economic nationalism in various parts of the world. Brexit in the UK and the independence movement in Catalonia are recent examples of attempts to break away from larger entities in search of greater autonomy. The European Union, created for the purpose of facilitating free economic and monetary exchange among its members, now faces significant challenges. However, the dominant media narrative often misleads society into believing that leaving a "group" is always a negative thing.

As in personal relationships, partnerships between countries should be based on mutual benefit. There is nothing healthier and more ethical than maintaining relationships with those who truly help us to grow and prosper. Globalisation should not be seen as a threat to national sovereignty, but as an opportunity to improve our lives through the exchange of ideas, goods and services.

Globalisation as a Tool for a Better Future

Globalisation is much more than an economic concept; it is the bridge that connects us to the knowledge, technology and resources needed to build a better future. Thanks to it, we can access life-saving medical technologies, medicines that cure diseases and solutions that improve our quality of life and increase our productive processes, increasing our levels of competitiveness. Rejecting globalisation is like closing the door to a world full of possibilities.

Instead of fearing it, we must learn to navigate the complex world of globalisation, understanding that it offers us the opportunity to grow, learn and prosper. Money and resources flow to where value and opportunity are generated. If we are able to adapt, innovate and collaborate, globalisation will not be a threat, but a blessing.

Globalisation is not a bad thing; it is a powerful force that, when managed wisely, can lead us to a future of greater prosperity and well-being. It allows us to share humanity's achievements and advances, to access technologies that improve our lives, and to collaborate in building a more connected and efficient world. Globalisation is the engine that drives innovation, collaboration and progress.

Of course, globalisation is not without its challenges. It requires careful management, policies that ensure that benefits are distributed equitably, and a commitment to ethics and sustainability. But, at the end of the day, it is our best chance to build a future in which we can all prosper.

Instead of demonising globalisation, we must embrace it intelligently, ensuring that its benefits reach everyone and using its tools to build a fairer, more equitable and prosperous world.

Expanding the Vision: A Call to Action

To gain a true understanding of globalisation and its benefits, it is necessary to broaden our vision beyond national borders and look to the future with an open mind. The challenge is not to stop globalisation, but to manage it so that its benefits are distributed fairly and equitably. Globalisation can be a tool to reduce poverty, improve access to education and health, and foster innovation in every corner of the globe.

It is essential that world leaders, business people and ordinary citizens understand that globalisation is not a zero-sum game, where some win and others lose. It is a dynamic process that, when properly managed, can raise living standards for all participants. But for this to happen, it requires a genuine commitment to social justice, business ethics and international cooperation.

We are at a turning point in history, where we can choose to embrace globalisation and its benefits, or retreat into a world of closed borders and isolation. The choice is ours, and the consequences of that choice will determine the course of our society for generations to come.

A Global Future: The Promise of International Collaboration

Imagine a world where trade barriers are lowered, ideas flow freely and knowledge is shared without restriction. A world where each country brings its best to the table, not just for its own benefit, but for the good of all humanity. This is the world that globalisation promises us, a world where international collaboration is not only desirable, but essential to our survival and prosperity.

Instead of seeing globalisation as a threat, we should see it as an opportunity to build a brighter and more equitable future. It is a call to action for each of us to play our part in creating a more connected world, where knowledge, technology and resources are available to everyone, wherever they live.

Globalisation is the tool that can lead us to a better future, but only if we are willing to embrace it responsibly and wisely. It is our task to ensure that this process is used to improve the lives of all, not just a few. If we get it right, globalisation will not be seen as a destructive force, but as the key that opens the door to a future of hope, progress and shared well-being.

CHAPTER 8

WORLD ECONOMY: THE TRUE FACE OF THE GLOBAL GAME

CHAPTER 8

WORLD ECONOMY: THE TRUE FACE OF THE GLOBAL GAME

When I attended World Economics classes during my undergraduate studies, I always wondered what was the difference between Microeconomics and Macroeconomics. These two branches of economics were often mentioned, but for a long time, their distinction seemed abstract, almost intangible to me. It was only after several years of reflection, at the end of that stage of my training, that I realised that the difference between the two lies in a question of scale: the zeros to the right of each number. In other words, if you understand the sum of 1 - 1, you understand the sum of 1,000,000,000,000,000,000,000 - 1,000,000,000,000,000,000. The result is still zero. That revelation made me understand that economic principles are universal, applicable to a small business as well as to the economy of an entire nation.

With this understanding in mind, it is clearer for me to analyse the economy of a country like Spain, the place where I was born. Spain, a nation with a developed economy, can serve as an example to understand the real situation of its economy and, by extension, that of any other country. I invite you to carry out a similar analysis with your own country and compare it with others, so that you can better understand what we will discuss below. (Personally, I have learned a lot by using the data comparator at datosmacro.expansion.com. From here, thank you).

What is the real situation of the Spanish economy?

To understand a country's economy, it is essential to compare its macroeconomic data with those of other nations. Let's take Spain as a reference and compare its situation with that of two countries that are very different in size and economic situation: Qatar and Singapore. Qatar and Singapore are two of the richest countries in the world, while the United States is one of the largest and most powerful economies on the planet. I have recently had the opportunity to visit these countries and learn first-hand about their different economic perspectives.

Comparison: Spain vs Qatar

Data from 2018 (pre Pandemic crisis)

Let us look at the first comparison: Spain versus Qatar. Qatar, a country with only 2,780,000 inhabitants, has a positive trade balance of +33,573,000,000 euros. On the other hand, Spain, with more than 46,934,632 inhabitants, i.e. a population almost 17 times larger, has a negative Trade Balance of -36,399,000,000,000 euros. It is surprising that Qatar, with a much smaller population, maintains such a high positive trade balance, while Spain, with a considerably larger population, is in the red.

This contrast reveals one of the main problems of economies with negative balance sheets: **lack of competitiveness.** As a society, we have not been trained to take individual responsibility for generating something that can be sold and, in return, enjoy a life full of resources. Here I want to clarify something: the term "selling" is often confused with capitalism, but selling is nothing more than generating a value-added good that brings a benefit to others. Whether it is selling food in the Neolithic era, such as cows, potatoes or lettuce to feed the rest of the population, or developing a cancer drug in the 21st century.

In short, what is often confused with ambition for power, and which certainly can be if misdirected, is nothing more than the effort of each individual to bring added value to humanity in order to improve the quality of life of others. This is a task that every human being must develop in order to be able to exchange goods and services and thus meet his or her own needs.

The gulf between Spain and Qatar

The abysmal difference between Spain and Qatar lies mainly in the amount of goods that each country generates and exports. Qatar, a major producer of liquefied natural gas, has managed to far outstrip its imports. Thanks to its ability to transport gas in liquid form (by cooling it to temperatures below minus 160 degrees Celsius), Qatar supplies heating and transport to millions of homes around the world.

This balance of trade success is not only due to Qatar's natural resources, but also to its ability to innovate and develop technologies that allow it to maximise the value of these resources. Its economy is built on a solid foundation of exporting high-value goods, which contrasts sharply with the Spanish economy, which is still struggling to find a balance between imports and exports.

Another noteworthy fact is its level of debt, which we will analyse in more detail in the next chapter. Although Qatar has a higher per capita debt than Spain, the management of this debt is completely different. While debt in countries with weak economies is often a burden that limits growth and development, in Qatar, debt is managed strategically, investing in infrastructure and projects that generate long-term economic returns.

In terms of Gross Domestic Product (GDP) per capita, Qatar is surprisingly more than twice as high as Spain, with almost zero unemployment, close to full employability and generating jobs for its almost 2 million immigrants, double the national population. This also contrasts with Spain's historically high unemployment rate.

Qatar's public spending per capita is almost double that of Spain. However, unlike Spain, Qatar's main investment is in the production of goods of public interest that attract tourism and generate significant revenue for the country. This approach allows it to provide services to its citizens without resorting to an increase in negative debt, but rather by managing positive debt, earmarked for productive investment. Qatar has been able to take advantage of its natural resources and strategic position to build a diversified economy that is resilient to global market fluctuations.

Comparison: United States vs Singapore

Now, let us consider the comparison between the United States and Singapore. Despite being one of the world's major powers, the United States has one of the largest debts in the world. To put it in perspective, every baby born in the US is greeted with an inherited debt of €53,233.46 per child, and rising steadily, probably well above this figure today. And this is not just any debt, but negative debt, debt that fails to greatly increase their ability to generate a significant increase in wealth, but represents a liability that limits future opportunities. This growing debt is a reflection of America's tendency to finance its lifestyle and global position by issuing debt, rather than generating wealth through production and export.

Singapore, on the other hand, has a small economy compared to the United States, but has proven to be much more efficient in managing its economy. Despite its size, Singapore has managed to maintain a trade surplus and sustained economic growth, thanks to export-oriented policies and the attraction of foreign investment. Singapore has become a global hub for technology, finance and trade, demonstrating that a small economy can be hugely competitive if managed properly.

Results of the Income - Expenditure equations

Let's examine the current income-expense equations for the countries mentioned:

- **Spain:** -30.495.000.000 €.
- **Qatar:** +8.564.000.000 €.
- **United States:** -989,710,000,000 €.
- **Singapore:** +11.194.000.000 €.

Another of the main hidden problems of negative performing economies is their strategy of more money circulation in order to repay their debt. In the case of the US, its main global deception is to put more money into circulation, while trying to maintain the value of its currency through an artificial demand for foreign exchange as a benchmark in international trade relations. This approach is aimed solely at covering the huge debt repayments accumulated by decades of deficits. However, this system is unsustainable in the long run and creates a bubble that, at any moment, can burst.

If the United States begins to lose its strength as the world's exchange currency, its global market could collapse. The reason is that there is no true relationship between the amount of goods generated and the amount of banknotes printed. This creates a situation where, although there is more money in circulation, that money has no real value to back it up, eventually leading to devaluation and economic crises. This risk is particularly high when confidence in the currency begins to erode, which can trigger a massive sell-off of assets denominated in that currency, accelerating the collapse.

Supply and demand: the real value of goods

To better understand this process, let's consider the principle of supply and demand. Imagine you have an asset, such as a house, that you want to sell for €150,000. The real value of that house is not determined by you, but by the market, depending on how many people are interested in buying it and how many similar houses are available. If demand is high and supply is low, the price will go up, but if the opposite is true, the price will go down. This is the same principle that governs the value of currencies in the international market.

The same principle applies to a country's currency. The value of currency depends on supply and demand. When a country prints more money without a real relationship to the goods produced and without sufficient demand for that currency, the whole system risks collapse. In short, printing more money without a solid basis in the real economy is a recipe for disaster. This is particularly dangerous in a globalised world, where currencies are interconnected and the collapse of one major currency can have knock-on effects on other economies.

In conclusion, we have analysed the differences between countries with positive and negative economies, using examples such as Spain, Qatar, the United States and Singapore. We have seen how mismanagement of the economy and the creation of debt without productive backing can lead to unsustainable situations in the long run. We have also learned that the real value of goods and currencies is determined by supply and demand, and that any attempt to manipulate this balance by printing money or accumulating debt without a sound basis is doomed to failure.

It is essential that we understand these dynamics if we are to have a clear view of the real world economy and make informed decisions in our own lives. We must be aware of the risks inherent in a global economy that depends as much on trust and perception as it does on the actual production of goods and services. In the next chapter, we will take a closer look at debt analysis and how debt management can make the difference between a thriving economy and one in decline.

I take this opportunity to invite you to explore the videos available on YouTube from the Visualpolitik team. Through their content, you will have the opportunity to immerse yourself in a detailed and visually engaging analysis of the evolution of different countries over time. These videos offer an in-depth and well-documented perspective on how economic, social and geopolitical policies have shaped the development of various nations, allowing you to better understand the global dynamics that influence today's world.

Visualpolitik stands out for its ability to break down complex issues into accessible and easy-to-understand formats, using graphics, interactive maps and well-structured narratives. This will allow you to not only absorb information more effectively, but also to see how historical trends connect to current and future events.

By watching these videos, you will be able to broaden your understanding of how factors such as globalisation, government policies, international conflicts and technological innovations have impacted the trajectory of different economies and societies. This knowledge is not only valuable for understanding the past and present, but also for anticipating possible future scenarios in a world that continues to change rapidly.

I encourage you to take the time to enjoy these resources and to reflect on patterns and lessons that can be applied to your own life and strategic decisions. With Visualpolitik, you will have a powerful tool to increase your global vision and improve your analytical skills in an increasingly interconnected context.

Thank you to the Visualpolitik team for the excellent work you do. Your dedication to providing high quality content and your ability to tackle complex issues in a clear and concise manner is truly admirable. Keep up the great work!

CHAPTER 9

LESSONS OF WEALTH: THE PHENOMENON OF DUBAI, QATAR OR SINGAPORE

CHAPTER 9

LESSONS OF WEALTH: THE PHENOMENON OF DUBAI, QATAR OR SINGAPORE

The story of Dubai, Qatar and Singapore is a powerful lesson in how vision, strategic planning and determination can transform territories with humble beginnings into global economic giants. Although these three places are separated by thousands of miles and have very different historical and geographical contexts, they share a common narrative: the ability to overcome adverse circumstances and emerge as economic powerhouses in a competitive, globalised world.

Dubai: From Desert to Global Metropolis

Dubai, one of the seven emirates that make up the United Arab Emirates, is an iconic example of how vision and leadership can transform a desert region into one of the world's most advanced and vibrant cities. Located on the coast of the Persian Gulf, Dubai was, until the mid-20th century, a small fishing port whose main resource was pearl fishing. That all changed in 1966, however, when oil deposits were discovered. Although oil wealth was the initial catalyst for its development, Dubai was not content to rely solely on this resource.

Dubai's real transformation began in the 1980s under the leadership of Sheikh Mohammed bin Rashid Al Maktoum, who looked beyond oil and sought to diversify the emirate's economy. Under his leadership, Dubai began to invest heavily in infrastructure, tourism, finance and trade. The creation of the Jebel Ali Free Zone in 1985 was a turning point, attracting thousands of international companies thanks to its tax incentives and lack of restrictions on foreign ownership.

One of the most criticised and, at the same time, least understood aspects of the Dubai model is its low taxation. Dubai has positioned itself as a tax haven, which has attracted many companies and entrepreneurs from around the world seeking an environment where their investments can flourish without the burden of high taxes. Unlike many economies that levy high taxes on corporate and personal profits, Dubai has opted for a low-tax strategy that, instead of scaring away investors, has encouraged large-scale business development thanks to its legal certainty. This model has enabled Dubai to become a global financial centre, where the ease of doing business is one of the best in the world.

Dubai's low taxation has been key to attracting not only businesses, but also international talent, who see the emirate as an opportunity to grow and prosper without the pressure of high taxes. Moreover, this policy has allowed Dubai to reinvest the revenues generated by its booming economy into world-class infrastructure, further strengthening its position as a global business and tourism hub.

Dubai has also positioned itself as a luxury tourist destination. The construction of the Burj Al Arab, one of the world's most luxurious hotels, and the Burj Khalifa, the world's tallest building, are just a few examples of how Dubai has used architecture and innovation to attract tourists from all over the world. In addition, Dubai has developed world-class infrastructure, including Dubai International Airport, which is one of the busiest airports in the world, and Jebel Ali Port, the largest port in the Middle East.

Another pillar of Dubai's success is its focus on technology and innovation. The emirate has invested significantly in the development of 'Smart Dubai', an initiative to make the city the smartest and most connected in the world, using advanced technologies such as blockchain, artificial intelligence and big data. Dubai has also launched "Dubai Internet City" and "Dubai Media City", special economic zones that have attracted tech giants and global media.

A key aspect of Dubai's success lies in its commitment to education and the resilience of its people. The emirate has made significant investments in state-of-the-art education systems, aligned with global trends, enabling its citizens to thrive in a dynamic and constantly evolving environment. I have been fortunate to witness this adaptability up close, thanks to my relationship with my great Emirati friend Badir, whose personal journey reflects Dubai's focus on preparing its people to be great leaders in the global economy.

Despite falling oil prices, Dubai has maintained steady economic growth, thanks in large part to its economic diversification and ability to adapt to new global trends. Today, Dubai is a global financial, tourism and technology hub, a testament to the power of vision and long-term strategic planning.

Qatar: From Fishing to Energy Prosperity

Qatar, a small country in the Persian Gulf, shares with Dubai a history of radical transformation. Until just over 50 years ago, Qatar was a country that barely scraped by on fishing and a modest pearl trade. But in 1971, the same year it gained independence from the UK, it was discovered that Qatar had vast reserves of oil and, later, natural gas under its soil. This discovery changed the country's fortunes forever.

Qatar's real treasure lies in the North Field, the world's largest natural gas field, discovered in the 1970s. Unlike oil, natural gas had no immediate value due to technological limitations in transportation, as it could only be moved through pipelines. However, in 1995, Emir Hamad bin Khalifa Al Thani took a gamble on an emerging technology: natural gas liquefaction, which allows the gas to be cooled to -161 degrees to turn it into a liquid and transported by sea. This gamble was a resounding success, and today Qatar is the world's largest exporter of liquefied natural gas (LNG).

Natural gas has provided Qatar with unprecedented wealth, but what sets Qatar apart is its focus on long-term investment. Qatar has used gas revenues to invest both domestically and abroad. Domestically, it has developed world-class infrastructure, including highways, ports, airports and research centres. Internationally, Qatar has acquired strategic assets around the world, becoming one of the largest investors in commercial property in cities such as London and New York, and in global companies such as Volkswagen, Barclays and Iberdrola.

Qatar's approach has been clear: invest in the future, diversify its economy and ensure that the wealth generated by natural resources is translated into sustainable development. This approach has enabled Qatar to maintain one of the most stable and prosperous economies in the world, despite fluctuations in oil and gas prices.

Singapore: From Slum to Global Powerhouse

Singapore, a small island state in Southeast Asia, is another impressive example of economic transformation. When Singapore gained independence from the British Empire in 1963, it was a country devastated by the Japanese occupation during World War II, with an economy dependent on low-productivity activities and a population living in extreme poverty. In 1965, Singapore seceded from Malaysia and became an independent nation, but with no natural resources and a fragile economy, its prospects did not look promising.

However, under Lee Kuan Yew's leadership, Singapore embarked on a path to prosperity that has made it one of the world's most successful and advanced economies. Lee understood that the only way to prosper was to integrate into the global market and attract foreign investment. To this end, the Singapore government adopted an entrepreneurial approach to running the country, establishing a legal and economic framework that facilitated the creation and operation of businesses.

Singapore focused on creating a business-friendly environment, with policies promoting competitiveness and economic openness. They limited the use of vehicles in the city to reduce pollution and congestion, and forced workers to save a significant portion of their income, creating a state fund that is used to cover health, education and retirement expenses. This fund has been efficiently managed by the government, which has used it to invest both at home and abroad.

Singapore's success is also due to its world-class education system, which has produced a highly skilled workforce. In addition, Singapore has developed an excellent healthcare system and has created an almost corruption-free environment, which has attracted businesses and professionals from all over the world.

Today, Singapore is a global industrial, commercial and financial centre, known for its high quality of life, low unemployment and impressive economic growth. It has shown that even a small country with no natural resources can become a global power if it adopts the right policies and focuses on innovation and competitiveness.

Lessons for the Rest of the World

The stories of Dubai, Qatar and Singapore offer valuable lessons for other countries, especially those struggling to find their place in the global marketplace. These three places have shown that, with the right strategy, even nations with few natural resources or unfavourable geographic conditions can achieve prosperity.

Dubai has shown how a country can transform itself into a global hub for tourism, finance and technology through economic diversification, investment in infrastructure and the implementation of a low tax policy that incentivises business development. Qatar has shown that natural wealth can be a springboard to sustainable stability and wealth if managed with vision and prudence. Singapore has shown that lack of natural resources is not an insurmountable barrier if policies of economic openness, competitiveness and fiscal responsibility are adopted.

A common element in the success of these three places is visionary leadership. Sheikh Mohammed bin Rashid Al Maktoum of Dubai, Emir Hamad bin Khalifa Al Thani of Qatar, and Lee Kuan Yew of Singapore all understood that long-term success requires bold decisions and strategic planning, and that the role of government is crucial in creating an enabling environment for economic development.

Comparing Dubai and Spain: The Benefits of Countries Considered Tax Havens

In a globalised world, a country's fiscal and economic competitiveness can determine the well-being and success of its population. So-called "tax havens", such as Dubai, not only stand out for their low tax rates, but also for their ability to offer a superior quality of life to their residents. Let's take a closer look at a detailed comparison between Dubai and Spain, focusing on how differences in tax policies, costs of living, and government structures impact both businesses and citizens. Let's discover how these characteristics make Dubai a role model and an attractive destination for both employers and workers.

1. Benefits for Companies

Dubai, considered a tax haven, offers a highly competitive environment for companies thanks to its low tax rates. Companies in Dubai enjoy significantly lower costs compared to countries such as Spain. This allows them to offer products and services at more competitive prices in the global market. The absence of corporate and personal taxes in many of Dubai's free zones reduces financial burdens, allowing companies to reinvest their profits and expand more quickly.

In contrast, Spain, with its high tax burden, imposes a more challenging environment for companies. The tax burden on companies and workers is considerably higher, which reduces the room for manoeuvre for companies and makes their products more expensive on the international market.

2. Comparison of Gross and Net Salaries

To better understand the difference between Dubai and Spain, let's compare a salary cost of €35,000 between the two countries:

In Spain:

1. **Total cost for the company:** 35.000€.

   o **Social Security payable by the Company:** Approximately 35% of gross salary.

- Gross salary of the worker: €25,926 (approximately).

2. **Worker's contributions:**

   - **Social Security payable by the worker:** Approximately 6.35% of gross salary, which would be €1,647.

   - **IRPF (Impuesto sobre la Renta de las Personas Físicas):** Approximately 18% of gross salary, resulting in €4,666 (varies according to personal and family situation).

3. **Worker's Net Wage:**

   - **After Social Security:** €24,279.

   - **After personal income tax:** €19,613 (approximately).

   - **Net Monthly Salary: 1.634€.**

In Dubai:

1. **Total cost for the company:** 35.000€.

   - **Gross salary of employee:** €35,000 (no social security contributions or income tax).

2. **Worker's contributions:**

   - **Social Security:** Not applicable.

   - **Income Taxes:** Not applicable.

3. **Worker's Net Wage:**

   o **Net Salary:** 35.000€.

   o **Net Monthly Salary: 2.916€.**

Comparison:

- **In Spain**, of the €35,000 labour cost, the worker receives a net monthly salary of **€1,634.**

- **In Dubai**, a worker receives a net monthly salary of **€2,916.**

This comparison shows that in Dubai, both the company and the employee enjoy a much more favourable tax environment. This translates into greater savings capacity and purchasing power for the employee in Dubai compared to Spain, where tax burdens and social contributions significantly reduce the net disposable salary.

3. **Additional taxes:**

In addition, all net salaries in Spain are fully taxed, as we will see below:

Indirect taxes

- **VAT (Value Added Tax):**

   o **General:** 21%.

   o **Reduced (food, medicines, transport, etc.):** 10%.

- Super-reduced (basic foodstuffs such as bread, milk, fruit, etc.): 4%.

Property and Vehicle Taxes

- **IBI (Impuesto sobre Bienes Inmuebles):** Varies according to the municipality, but is usually between 0.4% and 1.1% of the cadastral value.

- **Road tax:** Depends on the type and power of the vehicle, but can range from around €20 to more than €200 per year.

- **Registration Tax:** Varies according to the vehicle's emissions and can be from 0% to 14.75% of the vehicle's value.

Transaction Taxes

- **ITP (Impuesto sobre Transmisiones Patrimoniales):** Varies between 6% and 10% of the value of the property, depending on the autonomous community.

- **AJD (Actos Jurídicos Documentados):** 0.5% to 1.5% of the value of the deed, generally applied in the purchase of homes.

Service Fee

- **Rubbish Tax:** Varies according to the municipality, but is usually between €50 and €150 per year.

- **Electricity and Water Supply Tax:** Approximately 5% of electricity consumption for electricity taxes.

Comparison with Dubai

Most of these taxes do not apply in Dubai. Although there is a general VAT of 5% levied on certain goods and services, including food, there is no personal income tax, IBI (Real Estate Tax), road tax or vehicle registration tax. This absence of direct taxation provides greater savings capacity and a higher quality of life due to the lower tax burden compared to Spain. As a result, residents enjoy higher net incomes and lower costs for a large majority of essential services, which improves their purchasing power and allows for a more comfortable lifestyle.

4. Corporate Taxation between Dubai and Spain

In addition to all the tax costs analysed in the previous sections, companies are faced with the following tax comparison:

Corporate Taxation in Spain:

1. **General Type:**

   o **25%** of annual net profits.

2. **Reduced rates:**

   o **Newly created companies**: 15% for the first two years with a positive tax base.

3. **Maximum Type:**

- For large companies, the rate can go up to **35%** depending on additional deductions or surcharges in certain cases.

Example of Calculation in Spain:

- If a company has an annual profit of **€300,000**, the taxes payable would be:

  - **25% of €300,000 = €75,000.**

  - If you apply the maximum rate of **35%**, it would be **€105,000.**

Corporate Taxation in Dubai:

1. **General Rate Introduced in 2023:**

   - **0%** for income up to **AED 375,000** (approximately **€94,000**).

   - **9%** for income over **AED 375,000.**

Example of Calculation in Dubai:

- For an annual profit of **€300,000** (approximately **AED 1,200,000**):

  - **9%** of **AED 1,200,000** = **AED 108,000** (approximately **€27,000**).

Comparison:

- **In Dubai**, a company with an annual profit of **€300,000** would pay **€27,000** in taxes.

- **In Spain**, the same company would pay between **€75,000** (25%) and **€105,000** (35%) depending on the applicable rate.

Dubai's tax environment offers significant advantages in terms of tax costs, allowing companies to retain more of their profits, reinvest in growth and offer more competitively priced products in the global market. In addition, the absence of additional taxes and robust legal certainty make Dubai an attractive destination for entrepreneurs and investors.

4. Debunking Myths:
Health

There is a mistaken belief that tax havens do not care about the health of their citizens. In Dubai, although healthcare is not free, private health insurance offers excellent coverage at much lower costs compared to the taxes citizens pay for public healthcare in Spain. Dubai residents can access high-quality medical services through affordable insurance, which, combined with the absence of taxes, results in a more efficient and less burdensome system. In contrast, in Spain, public healthcare is financed through high taxes, which significantly reduces the take-home pay available to citizens.

Education

Education in Dubai also follows a largely private model, where schools and universities are mostly of high quality, with a focus on academic excellence and preparation for a global market. Families can choose from a wide range of institutions to suit different needs and budgets. Although education comes at a cost, tax-free income makes it easier for families to meet these expenses. In Spain, public education is funded by high taxes, which, while ensuring universal access, may imply limitations in terms of resources and educational quality compared to Dubai's private system.

Pensions

The pension system in Dubai is different from that in Spain. Dubai does not have a public pension system as in Spain, where workers and employers contribute during working life to receive a pension in retirement. Instead, Dubai residents have the possibility to manage their savings independently or through private investment funds, allowing more control over their future income. In Spain, pensions are insured by the state, but the sustainability of the system is an issue of concern due to fiscal pressure and an ageing population.

Cost of Living and Saving Capacity

Contrary to another common myth, the cost of living in Dubai, including housing and food, is not necessarily higher than in Spain. In fact, the high savings capacity of workers in Dubai, thanks to the almost complete retention of their income, allows them to enjoy a high standard of living without the heavy tax burdens found in other countries.

Government and Economic Structure

Dubai's success is largely due to its government, which acts as an independent economic structure capable of generating value and financing itself without the need to exert high fiscal pressures on its citizens. This model allows the government to provide high-quality infrastructure and services without relying on traditional taxation. In addition, Dubai has created an environment that promotes productivity and commitment in both the public and private sectors, with politicians demonstrating exemplary loyalty and efficiency.

Security and Talent

Dubai offers a secure legal structure that guarantees the protection of citizens' and businesses' rights, which is fundamental to its prosperity. In contrast, Spain faces significant challenges in this regard. The lack of a favourable and secure economic environment in Spain is leading to a talent drain, with skilled professionals emigrating in search of better working and economic conditions, such as those offered by Dubai.

Final analysis

In Dubai, as in most places considered tax havens, the tax structure allows citizens and residents to enjoy higher net salaries due to the absence of direct income taxes. This gives them greater ability to purchase health services, education and manage their savings privately and efficiently. In Spain, although these services are largely guaranteed by the state, the high taxes needed to finance them significantly reduce citizens' purchasing power. This structure imposes an additional burden on businesses and workers, severely limiting and damaging their ability to save and invest personally.

Dubai presents a model where the government generates its own revenues through value creation rather than imposing high tax burdens on its citizens, thus enabling a more favourable environment for savings, investment and personal growth. This model, combined with a secure legal structure and efficient public policies, makes Dubai an attractive location for both businesses and individuals seeking to maximise their financial well-being and quality of life. In contrast, Spain faces significant challenges in terms of tax burden, sustainability of the pension system and the ability to deliver high quality services without compromising the take-home pay of its citizens.

In short, the reality of countries considered tax havens, such as Dubai, is that they offer numerous benefits for both companies and workers, thanks to their focus on economic efficiency, low tax burden, and legal certainty. These factors allow Dubai to create an environment where talent and investment can flourish, in contrast to all the economic and fiscal difficulties currently faced by countries with contrary policies, such as Spain, which are considered tax havens that favour the purchasing power and quality of life of their citizens.

CHAPTER 10

PAY, SAVINGS AND RETIREMENT: REDEFINING THE FINANCIAL FUTURE

CHAPTER 10

PAY, SAVINGS AND RETIREMENT: REDEFINING THE FINANCIAL FUTURE

For many years, my grandfather reminded me, during our long days of labouring in the fields, that he had never gotten rich with the strategy of being a worker who, through his daily efforts, relied solely on his salary and his ability to save to reach retirement with a rich retirement. This advice resonated with me over time, especially as I observed the economic realities we face today. My grandfather often mentioned the huge difference in the increase in prices of goods and services and how little wages and retirement benefits had increased, even though today they may be linked to increases in the same proportion as increases in the term we know as the CPI (Consumer Price Index).

What is really going on?

To understand my grandfather's concern, we must first analyse what has changed in recent decades. In the old days, the relationship between salary, cost of living and savings was more balanced. People could expect that, with a stable job, steady savings and a frugal life, they would achieve a comfortable retirement. However, this formula seems to have become less effective over time.

One of the most important factors to consider is wage stagnation. While prices of goods and services have risen dramatically, real (inflation-adjusted) wages have remained almost static. This situation has led to a widening gap between the cost of living and incomes, making it more difficult for people to save and secure a comfortable retirement.

Moreover, pension and retirement systems, once considered sound and reliable, are under increasing pressure due to factors such as ageing populations, globalisation and recurrent economic crises. This means that people who rely solely on their salaries and pensions may find that their savings are not sufficient to maintain their standard of living in retirement.

Why is there such a difference?

To understand why there is such a large gap between price increases and wage growth, we need to delve deeper into the nature of inflation and how it affects purchasing power.

1. Inflation and its real impact:

Inflation is the general increase in the prices of goods and services in an economy. In theory, wages should rise in line with inflation so that people's purchasing power remains stable. In practice, however, this rarely happens. Wages often do not grow at the same rate as inflation, leading to a decline in purchasing power. There are several reasons for this phenomenon:

- **Inequality in the distribution of wealth:** As wealth becomes concentrated in the hands of the few, working class wages tend to stagnate. Employers may not have the incentive to raise wages if they have access to cheap and abundant labour.

- **Rising costs of essential goods and services:** While some goods and services may remain stable in price, others, such as housing, education and health care, have risen much faster than overall inflation. This means that, although the CPI reflects a moderate increase in prices, the real costs faced by individuals have grown significantly more.

- **Loss of workers' bargaining power:** In recent decades, trade unions have seen a decline in their influence, which has negatively affected their ability to negotiate meaningful wage increases for workers. Instead of focusing on strategies that promote productivity and improve business performance, they have opted for approaches that often reduce efficiency, discourage labour engagement and prioritise shorter working hours. This approach has also contributed significantly to the failure of wages to keep pace with inflation, affecting workers' purchasing power.

- **2. Real inflation and the loss of purchasing power:**

Official inflation, as measured by the CPI, does not always reflect the reality experienced by individuals. The goods and services used to calculate the CPI may not represent the most significant expenditures for individuals. For example, while the cost of electronics or clothing may have decreased or remained stable, the prices of housing, education and health care have risen considerably. This means that even if the CPI indicates low inflation, people may be experiencing a significant loss of purchasing power.

Loss of purchasing power is a serious problem because it directly affects people's ability to maintain their standard of living. When wages do not grow at the same rate as prices, people are forced to reduce their consumption, take on more debt or save less, which in turn affects their ability to prepare for retirement.

Why does the "study, work, save and retire" formula no longer work?

The classic formula of "study, work, save and retire" has long been the mantra of economic stability. However, in the modern economy, this formula has proven to be insufficient to guarantee a secure and comfortable retirement.

1. Changes in the labour market:

The labour market has changed dramatically in recent decades. Job stability is no longer guaranteed, and jobs for life are increasingly rare. People change jobs more frequently, often facing periods of unemployment or underemployment. In addition, the rise of the gig economy (temporary and freelance jobs) has meant that many workers do not have access to traditional employment benefits, such as pension plans and health insurance, further complicating the ability to save for retirement.

2. The inadequacy of traditional savings:

With low returns on savings accounts and inflation eroding purchasing power, traditional savings have lost much of their effectiveness as a tool for securing retirement. Even those who manage to save a significant portion of their salary may find that their purchasing power has declined dramatically by the time they retire.

3. Increased life expectancy:

People are living longer than ever before, which means they need to save more to cover a longer retirement period. However, few save enough to cover 20 or 30 years of retirement, leaving many people at risk of running out of funds in their later years.

The need to become an investor or entrepreneur

Given the current economic situation, it is more important than ever for people to consider other ways of securing their financial future. Relying solely on a salary and traditional savings is no longer sufficient. It is crucial to explore investment opportunities and consider entrepreneurship as a way to create multiple sources of income and build wealth that can be sustained over time.

1. Investment as a hedge against inflation:

Investing in assets that outpace inflation, such as real estate, stocks or mutual funds, can help protect and increase the value of money over time. Unlike money saved in low-interest accounts, investments have the potential to generate significant returns that can ensure a comfortable retirement.

2. Entrepreneurship as an additional source of income:

Becoming an entrepreneur not only allows people to generate additional income, but also gives them control over their financial future. Starting a business, even on a small scale, can be an excellent way to diversify income sources and reduce dependence on a single salary.

Historical World Inflation Developments

To understand the impact of inflation on our daily lives, it is crucial to examine how global inflation has evolved over the past five decades. Inflation, which measures the general increase in the prices of goods and services, has had a significant impact on people's ability to save and plan for their retirement.

Historical World Inflation Developments

Since the 1970s, headline inflation has experienced several phases marked by significant peaks and troughs. In the 1970s, inflation reached extremely high levels due to oil shocks and expansionary monetary policies. This period was followed by a gradual decline in the 1980s and 1990s, thanks to stabilisation policies implemented by several countries, including higher interest rates and control of the money supply.

During the early years of the 21st century, global inflation remained relatively low, except for a few spikes in specific countries. However, since the COVID-19 pandemic and the war in Ukraine, the world has again experienced a significant rise in inflation, reaching levels not seen since the 1970s.

World Inflation Developments (1970-2023)

To better understand how inflation has affected the global economy and, consequently, people's ability to save and plan for their retirement, it is useful to examine the evolution of global inflation over the past 50 years. However, it is crucial to bear in mind that the official inflation data that are published often understate the reality of the inflationary impact on people's purchasing power.

Historical World Inflation Data:

- **1970s**: This decade was marked by very high headline inflation, with rates in many countries officially exceeding **10% per annum.** However, when all factors of price increases in essential goods are taken into account, including the spillover effects of oil shocks, actual inflation experienced by consumers was significantly higher. In developed countries such as the US and many European nations, real inflation could have exceeded **15%** in several years of this decade, severely eroding purchasing power.

- **1980s**: The early 1980s still reflected the high inflation rates of the late 1970s. Although official figures indicated a reduction to levels between **3-5%** per year in many developed countries, increases in the costs of essential goods such as housing, education and energy suggest that real inflation for the average consumer was considerably higher.

- **1990s**: During the 1990s, economic stability and globalisation helped to keep inflation at lower levels according to official figures, averaging **2-3%** per year in many advanced economies. However, when these figures are adjusted to better reflect increases in essential living costs such as housing and health care, actual inflation was probably closer to **5%** per year, which still represented a steady erosion of purchasing power.

- **2000s**: Headline inflation remained low and stable in this decade according to official data, averaging between **2% and 4%**. However, increases in real estate prices, commodities and energy costs suggest that the actual inflation experienced by many consumers may have been closer to **6%** per year on average, making it difficult for many to keep pace with the cost of living.

- **2010s**: Following the 2008 financial crisis, official headline inflation remained unusually low, with concerns even about deflation in some regions. However, official data often did not fully capture increases in daily living costs such as education, health and housing, suggesting that actual inflation may have been considerably higher than reported, especially for middle and lower class families.

- **2020 and beyond**: The COVID-19 pandemic in 2020 brought with it an unprecedented set of economic challenges, with global inflation officially reported to reach rates of **4-7%** in many advanced economies in 2022. However, considering increases in energy, food and housing costs, actual inflation affecting the average consumer was likely to be much higher, easily exceeding **10%** in some cases.

Real Cumulative Impact and Loss of Purchasing Power

When we look at the real cumulative impact of inflation since 1970, it is clear that prices of essential goods and services have risen significantly more than official figures indicate. While official figures might suggest an average price increase of around **300-400%** over the last 50 years, in reality, many consumers have experienced cost of living increases in excess of **800-1000%**.

This dramatic increase in prices has caused a massive loss of purchasing power for those who have relied solely on their wages, which have often not kept pace with real inflation. While cumulative wage revisions over the same period have been much more modest, with a total increase of around **200-300%** in many cases, this means that workers have seen their purchasing power eroded significantly. In real terms, many workers today can buy less with their wages than their parents or grandparents could 50 years ago, despite wage increases.

Impact of Inflation on Savings and Pensions

Inflation, by eroding the purchasing power of money, poses a silent but significant threat to savings and retirement planning. As prices rise, each unit of currency loses its ability to purchase goods and services. This phenomenon has serious implications for those who have planned their retirement solely on the basis of savings and pensions.

1. Inflation and the Real Value of Savings:

Over time, inflation can drastically reduce the real value of savings. For example, if a person saves 100,000 euros at an inflation rate of 3% per year, in 24 years that 100,000 euros would only have the purchasing power of approximately 50,000 euros in today's terms. This means that, although the number in the bank account remains the same, what can be bought with that money decreases over time.

This effect is even more pronounced in periods of high inflation, such as those experienced in various parts of the world during the 1970s and more recently in some emerging economies. During such periods, inflation can exceed 10% per annum, causing money to lose its value even more rapidly.

2. The Risk of Pension Erosion:

Pensions, especially those that are not indexed to inflation, are particularly vulnerable. If a pension is set at a fixed amount and inflation increases, the pensioner will see his or her purchasing power decline year after year. Although some pensions are designed to adjust for inflation, these adjustments are often limited or delayed, meaning that beneficiaries can still lose financial ground.

Moreover, in many economies, governments have begun to adjust pensions less generously or change the rules on indexation to cope with fiscal pressures. This puts at risk millions of retirees who rely on a fixed income in their golden years.

3. Impact on Cost of Living:

The cost of living for retirees is also disproportionately affected by inflation. This is because a greater share of retirees' spending goes on essential needs, such as health care, housing and food, areas where inflation tends to be higher. For example, while technology and clothing may have experienced relatively modest price increases, the costs of health care, food and housing have risen significantly in many parts of the world, putting further pressure on retirees' budgets.

4. Inflation and Traditional Savings Instruments:

Traditional savings instruments, such as savings accounts and certificates of deposit, often offer returns that barely match or exceed inflation, and in some cases do not even reach inflation. This means that while the money in these instruments may grow nominally, in real terms it may be losing value.

For example, if a savings account offers a return of 1% per year in an environment where inflation is 3%, the saver is losing 2% of purchasing power each year. This can be devastating for someone who relies on those savings to fund their retirement.

5. Strategies to Mitigate the Impact of Inflation:

To protect against inflation, it is essential to diversify savings and investments. Here are some key strategies:

- **Investments in assets that outperform inflation:** Assets such as stocks, real estate and certain inflation-indexed bonds can offer some protection against inflation. These assets tend to increase in value over time, compensating for the loss of purchasing power of cash.

- **International diversification:** Investing in international markets can also offer additional protection, as inflation rates vary from country to country. In a global environment, diversifying investments across different geographies can help mitigate inflation risk in any specific economy.

- **Continuous re-evaluation of the retirement plan:** It is crucial to regularly review the retirement plan and make adjustments according to changing economic conditions. This includes recalculating the amount needed for retirement based on current and expected future inflation, and adjusting investments accordingly.

6. The Crucial Difference between Assets and Liabilities

When it comes to improving our financial situation and securing a more stable financial future, it is critical to understand the difference between assets and liabilities. This is a concept that many people overlook or misunderstand, and as a result, find themselves trapped in a cycle of lost purchasing power and financial stagnation.

1. What is an Asset?

In simple terms, an asset is anything that puts money in your pocket. Assets generate income directly or indirectly, which means that, over time, they can increase your net worth. Examples of assets include:

- Investments in stocks or bonds: These assets generate income through dividends, interest, or capital appreciation.

- Rental properties: Real estate that you rent out to others is an asset, as it generates a positive cash flow.

- Owning your own business: A business that you generate and control, and that produces a steady income, is one of the most powerful assets you can have.

- Intellectual property: Patents, copyrights, or royalties from books, music, or inventions, which generate passive income.

2. What is a Liability?

On the other hand, a liability is anything that takes money out of your pocket. Liabilities, rather than generating income, represent a cost that you have to cover on a regular basis. These expenses can be overt, such as debt payments, or more subtle, such as maintaining an asset that does not generate income. Examples of liabilities include:

- **Mortgages or loans:** If you have a mortgage on your main home, even if you are paying for a property, this monthly expense is a liability if the house does not generate income for you.

- **Personal cars:** A car is a classic example of a liability. Although necessary for transportation, it loses value over time and requires constant expenses such as petrol, maintenance, and insurance.

- **Credit cards and personal debts:** Any debt that generates interest payments represents a liability.

3. The Common Mistake: Confusing Assets with Liabilities

One of the most common mistakes people make is confusing liabilities with assets. For example, many people consider their home to be their biggest asset. However, if the house you live in does not generate income, it is actually a liability. This is because it requires ongoing mortgage payments, taxes, insurance, and maintenance, without producing any positive cash flow.

This misunderstanding leads many people to over-invest in assets that are actually liabilities, resulting in a weaker financial position than they might have if they had invested in real assets.

4. The Importance of Investing in Real Assets

To break out of the vicious cycle of losing purchasing power, it is crucial to focus on acquiring and developing assets that actually generate income. Here's why this is so important and how you can do it:

- Generating passive income: A true asset not only maintains its value over time, but also generates passive income. This is income that you receive without having to actively work for it, such as rental property or stock dividends. The more of these assets you acquire, the more passive income you will have, allowing you to live with greater financial security and less stress.

- Appreciation in value: Many assets, such as shares or real estate, tend to increase in value over time. This means that not only will you earn income while you own the asset, but you may also be able to sell it in the future for more than you originally paid, earning a capital gain.

- Inflation protection: Income-generating assets tend to maintain or even increase in value during periods of inflation. For example, property rents tend to rise with inflation, as do dividends from companies that can pass on increased costs to their customers.

- Diversification and risk reduction: Investing in a variety of assets can help you diversify your income sources and reduce risk. If one investment fails, others can continue to generate income. This approach decreases your dependence on a single source of income, such as a salaried job.

5. Create and Develop Assets: Your Own Business or Participation in Others

One of the most effective ways to build a real asset is through starting your own business. Starting a business allows you to have direct control over income generation and gives you the opportunity to scale and grow that income over time. Here's why this is so valuable:

- Total control: When you own your business, you have control over all major decisions, from how money is spent to how income is generated. This allows you to align your business with your personal financial goals.

- Growth potential: A business of one's own has the potential to grow and generate more and more income. In the early years, although it may require a significant investment of time and money, the potential for rewards is far greater than in most other investments.

- Diversification opportunities: Within a business, you can create multiple revenue streams. For example, if you have a retail business, you could expand into online sales, offer complementary services, or even franchise your business model.

In addition, participating in other early-stage companies can also be a lucrative strategy. Startups and small companies with high growth potential can offer investment opportunities that, while riskier, have the potential to generate significant returns. These investments can be transformed into real assets that provide you with income over time and help you build a diversified portfolio of income streams.

6. Caution in your Investments

Investing is one of the most effective strategies for increasing your wealth and achieving financial independence. However, it is crucial to approach every investment with an informed and cautious mindset. Before you make your first investment, regardless of the path you choose (whether it's building your own business, investing in the stock market, acquiring real estate, or any other type of asset), there are a number of considerations you should take into account to protect your capital and maximise your chances of success. Here are some key precautions you should always keep in mind:

- Every investment carries a risk of total loss

The first principle you must internalise is that any investment you make may result in a total loss of the capital invested. No investment, no matter how safe it may seem, is risk-free. Therefore, never invest money that you are not willing to lose. This understanding will allow you to make more balanced decisions and not get carried away by enthusiasm or external pressure.

- Take losses in your stride

Losses are an inevitable part of the road to financial success. Don't torture yourself when you face losses; instead, embrace them as learning experiences. The key is to analyse what went wrong and use that information to improve your future decisions. Remember, even the most successful investors have experienced failures, but what sets them apart is their ability to bounce back and move forward.

- Prioritise your basic needs

Before embarking on any investment, make sure your basic needs are met: food, shelter and health. These are the foundations on which you can build your financial success. If your essential needs are not secured, it is unlikely that you will be able to stay focused and patient while you wait for the results of your investments. In addition, time is a critical factor in financial success, so you must look after your well-being in order to sustain your investment over the long term.

- Develop healthy daily habits

Investment success depends not only on smart financial decisions, but also on a balanced lifestyle. It is essential that you develop and maintain daily habits that strengthen both your physical and mental health. Make time for proper nutrition, regular exercise, sufficient rest, and stress management.

Develop daily habits in which you define the specific tasks to be carried out at any given time. Many people make the mistake of operating on autopilot during the day, without stopping to reflect on possible solutions to the incidents that arise, committing the great mistake of postponing analysis for the night. The day is for action and the night is for rest. It is crucial that you balance your time correctly: work, family, leisure and rest must have specific schedules. Do not mix these times, as doing so will affect your ability to take full advantage of them and will unbalance both your body and your mind.

These practices will give you the energy and mental clarity you need to make informed and sustainable decisions. Like a pyramid, your life must be balanced in all its aspects to be solid and resilient to challenges.

- Understand well the difference between assets and liabilities

As we have seen above, although simple once identified, one of the most common mistakes is often confusing assets with liabilities. Always remember that an asset is something that puts money in your pocket, while a liability is something that takes money out of your pocket. Don't forget the example of the house you live in, although it is valuable, it is generally a liability because it requires ongoing expenses and does not generate income. In contrast, the same rental property becomes an asset when it provides you with regular income. It is critical to invest in what is truly considered an asset under this definition. Otherwise, you could be putting your money into what are actually liabilities, limiting your ability to build wealth.

- Build your business with a solid strategy

If you decide to start and build your own business, it is crucial that you use the best strategies to compete with large companies. This includes thoroughly researching your market, identifying competitive advantages, and making sure you have a solid financial plan. A business built without a robust strategy will be at a disadvantage and could quickly fail.

- Invest only in what you understand

Never invest in something you do not fully understand. If someone presents an investment to you in a complex and confusing way, consider this a warning sign. The most successful investments are often easy to understand. If you can't clearly explain how an investment will work or how it will generate income, it's best to refrain.

- Investments are not a lottery

Investments are not an overnight rich scheme. It is more like a crop, where you must first prepare the soil, sow, water and care for the plants before you can harvest the fruits. Patience and perseverance are essential in the investment world. Sustainable and significant gains take time.

- Don't invest money you need in the short term.

You should always invest only the money you will not need in the short term. Investments, especially high-yield investments, often require time to mature and generate returns. If you invest money that you may need soon, you may be forced to sell at a bad time, which could result in losses.

- Be wary of investments that promise quick returns

If an investment promises quick and easy returns, it is probably not a good choice. Real investments take work and dedication to make money grow. Be wary of promises of big returns with little effort.

- Prioritise the team over the product

When evaluating an investment, especially in businesses or startups, prioritise the quality of the team. A product or service may look promising, but if the team behind it is not competent or is poorly managed, the chances of success are drastically reduced. Investing in capable and committed people is a safer strategy than relying solely on the attractiveness of the product.

- The stock market is not a game of chance

Don't invest in the stock market in the hope of making money by buying and selling stocks in the short term - that's not investing, that's speculation. Instead, if you decide to invest in the stock market, focus on companies with a strong track record of dividend payouts and look at these investments with a long-term perspective. Like the rich, invest in the stock market when others are panic selling, and pull out when the majority gets greedy.

- Don't be fooled by high dividends

High dividends are not always a sign of a safe investment. Sometimes companies raise their dividends when they are in financial difficulty to attract investors, which can be a sign that they are in urgent need of cash. It is wiser to invest in companies with consistent and reasonable dividends than in those that offer high yields with hidden risks.

- Make sure your investments outpace inflation

An investment that does not outpace the rate of inflation is actually a loss. For example, if a dividend yields you 3% but inflation is 5%, you are losing 2% of purchasing power each year. It is essential that your investments generate a net return that exceeds inflation so that you can maintain and grow your wealth.

- Calculate your own personal inflation rate

Don't blindly rely on official inflation rates. These figures often do not reflect the true cost increases you face in your daily life. A more accurate method is to calculate your own personal inflation rate, based on the rising prices of the goods and services you consume regularly, such as food, housing, and energy. This approach will give you a clearer picture of the actual inflation you are experiencing.

- Be wary of bank pension schemes

Many pension plans offered by banks do not guarantee returns above inflation, and some do not even guarantee that you will get back the full amount invested. It is vital to carefully analyse the terms and conditions of any pension plan before investing, and look for alternatives that offer better protection against inflation.

- Avoid bank deposits with low yields

Bank deposits that offer low yields, such as 2%, while banks lend that money at much higher rates, only benefit the financial institution, not you. While the bank sells your money to a third party at an average interest rate of 5%, they make a profit margin of 3% or more, while you are losing purchasing power because the return they offer is below average inflation. It is preferable to always look for investment alternatives that offer an adjusted return above inflation.

- Don't wait until you have 100% of the capital to invest.

Waiting until you have 100% of the necessary capital to start a project is a strategy that rarely works. In most cases, it is more effective to look for investors or partners who share your vision. Present your project to people you trust and seek their financial support. Remember that entrepreneurial success usually requires a team, and it is difficult to achieve great things alone. Do not get frustrated if you do not manage to attract a large investment initially, probably your environment does not have a large investment capacity and you will have to make important decisions that may involve changing your current residence, but believe me, the world is very big and there are many people who are willing to support, collaborate and invest in successful projects.

Never stop! Not in the face of anything or anyone. And always remember that most people who tell you that they don't see possibilities for your project are not talking about your limitations, but about their own.

CHAPTER 11

YOUR PERSONALITY, YOUR FORTUNE: THE BUSINESS REFLECTED IN YOU

CHAPTER 11

YOUR PERSONALITY, YOUR FORTUNE: THE BUSINESS REFLECTED IN YOU

After having faced a hard time in my life with the first tumour located in the spinal canal, I was diagnosed with hypogonadism as a consequence of another operation for testicular cancer, experiencing firsthand what sudden ageing means. My once strong and resilient body virtually stopped producing testosterone, and the consequences of this loss were devastating. Over the years, my brain lost many of its capabilities: concentration became an almost impossible task, anxiety episodes became constant and crippling, muscle strength faded, sex drive disappeared, and my mental security eroded to the point of almost disappearing. I even experienced cardiovascular problems that prevented me from climbing simple stairs. Everyday activities such as reading became a monumental challenge; I found it impossible to understand two paragraphs in a row. I avoided common situations like standing in line at the bakery or sitting at the hairdresser's because the anxiety they generated was simply overwhelming. I even lost the ability to perform one of my most cherished activities: driving. My neural ability to assess dimensions and calculate distances between vehicles around me was so impaired that I could no longer correctly judge the proximity between lanes and the ends of the road. This loss not only impacted my mobility, but also made me aware of how fragile our spatial perception is and how much we depend on it for our daily activities.

This has led me to discover in a much deeper and more scientific way the direct relationship between our chemical reactions and the people we become through the patterns we follow in our daily decision making, which define our path in life. This understanding is not limited to superficial intuition, but is based on a detailed analysis of how hormones, neurotransmitters and other biochemical factors influence every aspect of our being.

I have learned how testosterone, one of the most crucial hormones in the human body, influences a variety of biological processes that are fundamental to our physical and mental health and behaviour. Its impact goes far beyond what is commonly associated with this hormone, such as the development of secondary sexual characteristics. Testosterone is essential in the assimilation of cellular nutrients, in protein uptake by cells, and in the functionality of ATP (adenosine triphosphate), which is the main source of energy in our cells.

Testosterone plays a key role in neurotransmitters, which depend on this hormone to communicate properly. It affects the production and release of neurotransmitters such as dopamine and serotonin, which are involved in regulating mood, motivation and general well-being. In both men and women, the hormonal balance of testosterone, along with other hormones such as oestrogen, progesterone and oestradiol, plays a crucial role in health. An imbalance in hormone levels can lead to alterations in these neurotransmitters, which may explain why hormonal fluctuations are often linked to changes in mood and decision-making ability.

I have also come to the conclusion that it is imperative to make a significant improvement in our health care system, which should incorporate regular analysis and monitoring of hormone levels. This is necessary at all ages and especially crucial during the ageing process, when hormone production decreases prematurely in both men and women, in contrast to the increasing life expectancy we have achieved in recent decades. Despite this advance in longevity, our biological evolution has not yet fully adapted to these new realities, highlighting the need for hormone replacement therapies. These therapies could extend the quality of life of older people, preserving many of their functional capacities and preventing diseases that are directly caused by these hormonal imbalances.

In addition, it is essential that we move towards the manufacture of hormones specifically designed to meet the individual genetic requirements of each person. Personalised hormone production, tailored to the particular needs of each individual, could significantly minimise the side effects currently associated with generic hormones, which are not fully adapted to the unique characteristics of each human being. This approach would not only improve the efficacy of hormone therapies, but would also represent a crucial step towards a more precise and personalised medicine that responds to the specific demands of each patient and allows for a longer, healthier and fuller life.

After understanding all this, I was reminded of the urgent need for our society to continue to recognise the effort and full dedication we must make as a generation more responsible for creating a better world. Our health science is still light years away from discovering all that it needs to understand. It is disturbing to observe how many human mental health problems are treated, as mine was initially treated, with a chemistry that does nothing more than mask the real problem that may exist in our metabolism and thus in the correct processing of information through our brains.

Mental health, like physical health, depends on a delicate balance of biochemical processes. Approaching mental disorders from a pharmacological perspective alone is insufficient; a holistic understanding is needed that considers how diet, exercise, stress and other environmental factors, and even in many cases individual endogenous production - that which our own organs produce insufficiently or in the wrong chemical formulation - influence our metabolic, hormonal and neurological balance. Scientific understanding of these interactions may lead us to develop more effective treatments that not only treat the symptoms, but also address the underlying causes.

Scientific exploration of the relationship between our chemical reactions and our daily decisions has revealed a profound truth: our identity and the path we follow in life are shaped by complex and highly interrelated biochemical processes. Hormones play a multifaceted role in regulating our health and well-being. Understanding these processes at a deep level is essential not only to improve our physical health, but also to make more informed and responsible decisions that define our path in life. As a society, we must move towards a more integrated and comprehensive approach to health, one that recognises the interdependence of all the systems that make us up and enables us to build a healthier and more conscious future.

Today, although I have regained much of my functional capacity, I am not the same person I was before. However, if we analyse it, none of us is the same person we were the day before. Every experience lived, every challenge faced and every lesson learned transforms us, forging a new "me" in a process of continuous and permanent change.

Today, many policy proposals seek to incentivise basic incomes for people in vulnerable situations, even when these people are of sound mind. It is important to reflect on how this also affects mental health and each individual's commitment to a better society. Basic income, far from promoting personal growth, tends to discourage creativity and self-fulfilment. We all possess an innate talent, and finding and developing it is what really allows us to achieve happiness and personal fulfilment.

Providing basic incomes that only guarantee physiological needs may appear to be a support, but in reality, it is a detriment that holds back human potential. Solutions to economic imbalances must be addressed through education and the ability to generate added value for society. When governments choose to provide basic incomes instead of encouraging job creation through a strong education system, they are acknowledging their inability to generate job opportunities. These payments, instead of being a benefit, are a mechanism that keeps the population dependent and silent, without the necessary motivation to actively contribute to collective growth and well-being.

Moreover, these policies have serious economic consequences, as they increase the tax burden on the rest of the taxpayers and lead to currency devaluation. This economic imbalance arises because the economy is not supported by a population that keeps adding new goods and services, which is crucial for maintaining economic stability. Without constant value creation, these measures are not only unsustainable in the long run, but also weaken the overall economic structure, putting the well-being of society as a whole at risk.

Personality and its Impact on Business

Our personality is a complex product of our genetics and our life experiences. We are the sum of countless chemical reactions that affect our decisions, behaviours and perspectives. However, although our genetics predispose us to certain ways of being, we are not completely determined by them. We can modify, mould and develop our personality through constant inner work and continuous education. This rational part of us can be trained to guide our irrational part, which often acts on impulse, like chemical reactions in a laboratory.

One of the fundamental pillars of successful entrepreneurship is the development of a resilient and strong personality. An entrepreneur must become an indestructible being, someone who never gives up in the face of the obstacles that will inevitably arise along the way. This resilience must be accompanied by a positive mindset, where problems are redefined as incidences that can be solved. In fact, 99% of the challenges we face on a daily basis are not real problems, but manageable situations. Real problems are rare and are usually related to the loss of basic necessities of life, such as health or survival. Everything else has a solution, and our attitude towards these challenges is what really determines our success.

I remember how my father used to say to me when I was little: "Son, dying is a condition of being born. If you cannot die, it is because you have not been born. Cherish the great opportunity we have given you at birth, and remember that as long as you have life, there will be no death, and when death comes, there will be no life. These words have been a guide in my life, reminding me that the finiteness of life is what drives us to live it to the full, to develop all our capacities and abilities, and to strive to leave the world a better place than we found it.

Confronting Fear and Redefining Success

Fear is one of the biggest obstacles to success. It blocks our ability to think clearly and make effective decisions. However, when we realise that our goal is to solve issues, not insurmountable problems, our perspective changes. In fact, if there were no issues, many of us would be out of work. Every day, we face challenges that allow us to grow, learn and improve, raising our level of competence and bringing us one step closer to becoming true entrepreneurs.

One of the most common fears is the fear of dying in debt. This fear is rooted in a lack of financial education and a limited view of what debt really means in the business world. Large companies and successful entrepreneurs do not see debt as a negative thing; they use it as a strategic tool to grow and expand. Many small entrepreneurs, however, make the mistake of taking on small debts with short repayment terms, often jeopardising the viability of their businesses. These entrepreneurs play by the rules imposed by financial institutions, which seek to maximise their profits in the shortest possible time, without considering the long-term impact on the financed company, even though none of them follow in their own economic structure the priority strategy they sell to other companies.

The Corporate Structure: The Heart of the Business

When we are in the process of setting up a business, it is crucial to establish a solid structure that includes the following key departments:

- **Human Resources Department**: Responsible for managing talent, recruiting and retaining the people who will make the business thrive.
- **Purchasing Department**: Responsible for acquiring the materials and services necessary to operate.
- **Commercial Department**: The company's sales engine, responsible for generating revenue.
- **Marketing Department**: Fundamental for positioning the brand and attracting customers.
- **Control Department**: Ensures that all operations are carried out efficiently and effectively.
- **Prevention Department**: Deals with safety and risk prevention, protecting both employees and the company.

- **Logistics Department**: Manages the flow of products and services from the supplier to the customer.
- **Legal Department**: Protects the company's legal interests, ensuring compliance with regulations.
- **Accounting Department**: Keeps track of the finances, ensuring that the company is profitable and sustainable.
- **Finance Department**: Manages financial resources, ensuring that the company has the necessary capital to grow.

Of all these departments, the Finance Department is the most critical in the initial stages of setting up a company. Without financial resources, it is impossible to develop the rest of the departments. However, this is where many small entrepreneurs make their first big mistake: they automatically turn to financial institutions for capital, without considering other more strategic options. Large companies, those in the major stock market indices, do not rely exclusively on bank financing in the form of loans. Instead, they issue equity to raise the necessary resources, which allows them to build robust structures without draining their cash. A good friend of mine taught me that the main reason for bankruptcy in companies is not lack of business viability, but moments of illiquidity in their cash flow.

In business accounting, large initial outlays do not necessarily indicate that a business is not viable. In fact, that is why Negative Results of Previous Years (NPLR) were created, to offset the negative effects of the initial investments needed to start up a large machine. With proper management, these investments will eventually generate positive results.

Bank Financing vs Shareholder Formation

The old belief that a good product guarantees success is no longer sufficient. Without a proper business structure and sound economic viability, even the best product can fail. However, many entrepreneurs do not consider the option of forming a shareholding and, instead, mistakenly choose to start their businesses with traditional bank financing alone. Why is this? The answer lies in a psychological misperception.

When someone starts a business for the first time, in most cases they usually have an idea, but rarely have the confidence to share it with others and offer them the opportunity to be part of the project. Instead of seeing their idea as a viable business opportunity, they think: "Who is going to bet on this idea? Business, doesn't that sound bad? Putting money in? Oops, that sounds worse, because I don't have any money, which means I'm poor. Ask for money? But that's poor. Project? Maybe I have too many birds in my head. I'd better go to a financial institution that will only ask for a business plan and my last tax return.

This mentality leads many entrepreneurs to opt for bank financing as the only option, without stopping to consider that a structure formed by a group of partners could be much more beneficial for the economic viability of the company.

Comparison of Financial Strategies

Let's see how the accounting result of a business with an initial investment requirement of €300,000 would be projected, using two different strategic plans and analysing only its financial costs:

- **Business Plan with Bank Financing:**
  - Amount: €300,000.
  - Bank loan with 6-year financing and an interest rate of 5%.
  - Monthly fee: 4.831,48 €.
  - Total annual cost: 57,977.76 €.

- **Business Plan with Partners:**
  - Amount: €300,000.
  - Monthly fee: 0 €.
  - Total annual cost: 0 €.

In the first case, the company has to allocate a significant part of its revenues to debt repayment from day one. This not only reduces its liquidity, but also limits its ability to reinvest and expand. In case of low initial revenues, it may face serious viability problems.

On the other hand, in the second case, by not being obliged to make monthly payments, the company has greater financial flexibility. This allows it to reinvest all profits back into the business, either to expand, to improve its products or services, or simply to build a reserve fund. In addition, this strategy reduces the risk of insolvency and provides a financial cushion in case the business takes longer to get off the ground, as is often the case.

The main advantage of the second plan is that it allows for a more organic and sustainable growth of the business, avoiding the pressure of meeting fixed financial obligations, and increasing the likelihood of long-term success. **In addition, this advantage provides the structure necessary to build a solid medium-term capital base, ensuring that the business not only survives, but thrives in a competitive environment.**

Entrepreneurial Personality: Key to Success

The success of a business depends not only on the financial and organisational structure, but also, and to a large extent, on the personality of the entrepreneur. The ability to face challenges, maintain motivation and adapt to changing circumstances is what distinguishes successful entrepreneurs from those who fail. Personality, as mentioned above, is not a static attribute; it can and should be developed and strengthened over time.

An entrepreneur must be resilient, but also flexible. He/she must know when to persist and when to pivot. He or she must be willing to take calculated risks, but also to learn from mistakes. And above all, he or she must have a clear vision of what he or she wants to achieve, and the determination to keep going, even when the going gets tough.

Your Business is a Reflection of Your Personality

At the end of the day, your business is a direct reflection of who you are. Your strengths and weaknesses, your fears and ambitions, all manifest in the way you manage and run your business. That's why working on your personal development is not just a matter of individual well-being; it's an investment in the success of your business.

Don't be afraid to share your vision with others. A good entrepreneur knows that you can't do it all alone, and that long-term success depends on the ability to build a strong team and a solid structure. Just as globalisation connects us to worldwide resources and knowledge, collaboration within your business connects you to the people and resources you need to thrive.

Remember, fear of failure is natural, but it shouldn't stop you. Every incident is an opportunity to learn and grow, and every challenge overcome brings you one step closer to becoming the entrepreneur you've always wanted to be.

As my father taught me, never fear the sea, but never forget to maintain the respect for it that is necessary to learn to navigate it wisely.

CHAPTER 12

BUSINESS PSYCHOLOGY: BUILDING CHARACTER IN ADVERSITY

CHAPTER 12

BUSINESS PSYCHOLOGY: BUILDING CHARACTER IN ADVERSITY

Psychology is a fundamental pillar in the life of any entrepreneur. Mental and emotional fortitude is often what distinguishes successful entrepreneurs from those who succumb to challenges. This chapter explores how psychology affects business management and how developing a resilient mindset can be the key to navigating through the storms that inevitably arise on the road to success.

The Inner Battle: Fighting Adversity

As I mentioned earlier, over the years, I have experienced firsthand the difficulties that can arise when the mind and body seem to conspire against you. It is the result of primary hypogonadism, a condition that affects testosterone production and which has triggered a series of psychological and physical problems: anxiety, depression, fears, nervousness, lack of concentration, loss of reading ability, tachycardia, muscle weakness and joint pain.

These symptoms not only affected my health, but also tested my ability to carry on with my projects and responsibilities. As my body stopped producing testosterone naturally, I was forced to face a series of emotional and physical challenges that, at many points, threatened to paralyse my life. Anxiety became a constant companion, making even the simplest tasks, such as waiting in line or concentrating on reading, difficult. Depression darkened my days, making every morning a struggle to find the motivation to keep going.

However, despite these challenges, I have remained steadfast in my goal, driven by the desire to help others better understand money, economics and business management, so that they can build a fulfilling and resource-rich life. The most valuable lesson I have learned during this process is that while the mind can be our worst enemy, it can also become our greatest ally if we learn to manage it properly.

The Importance of Emotional Support

In this process, I have been profoundly fortunate to have the unconditional support of the most important person in my life: my life partner. Since I was nineteen, she has been my pillar, my guide and my strength. Her love, understanding and ability to see life in a positive light have been crucial in my recovery process and in my ability to move forward, even when everything seemed dark.

It is critical for any entrepreneur to recognise the importance of emotional support. Whether it is a life partner, a friend, a mentor or a mental health professional, having someone who can offer perspective, comfort and motivation in difficult times is essential. Loneliness is a silent enemy that can lead to burnout and hopelessness, so surrounding yourself with people who bring light and positivity is vital to maintaining the psychological strength needed to face the challenges of the business world.

My partner has not only supported me in my darkest moments, but has also been a constant source of inspiration. His university education in psychology, his experience, his ability to pick himself up after every fall, his unwavering optimism and his inner strength have been a role model for me. Thanks to her example, I have learned to see obstacles as opportunities to grow, to value every small triumph and, above all, to never give up. His presence in my life has taught me that, although the road may be hard, we are never truly alone in our struggles. Furthermore, I have realised that success depends not only on individual effort, but also on the ability of couples to keep their life and business goals fully aligned. This alignment is crucial to overcome the bumps in the road and achieve success together, thus strengthening not only the emotional bond, but also the basis of any shared project.

The Psychology of Entrepreneurship: Forging Indestructible Character

A great entrepreneur must be like a superhero: unstoppable, invincible and indestructible, able to move forward despite the storms. This metaphor is not exaggerated, as the entrepreneurial journey is full of obstacles that can seem insurmountable. However, those who manage to maintain a strong and resilient mindset are the ones who end up achieving success.

The story of the captain who burns his ships to make his soldiers understand that the only chance of getting out alive is to fight to the end is a powerful reminder of the importance of determination. In business life, this mindset is crucial.

When there is no option to retreat, when only forward movement is contemplated, a solution is more likely to be found, no matter how difficult the scenario.

Psychology is therefore the most essential tool that every entrepreneur must develop and apply on a daily basis. It is not only about being strong in the face of adversity, but also about being able to lead with empathy, motivate a diverse team and handle stress and uncertainty with grace.

In addition, it is crucial that entrepreneurs learn to manage fear, which is one of the most paralysing emotions. Fear of failure, rejection or uncertainty can stop many on their way to success. However, the key is to learn to use fear as an engine that drives forward, rather than allowing it to become a brake. The ability to face fear, to move forward in spite of it, is what differentiates successful entrepreneurs from those who never reach their true potential.

Team Synergy: Selecting and Empowering Talent

A successful entrepreneur must be concerned not only with his or her own mental toughness, but also with that of the team around him or her. One of the most important skills is the ability to identify and nurture talent within the organisation. It is essential to learn to value the people who bring positive value and to weed out those who may be a burden to the team.

Albert Einstein said: "We are all very ignorant, but we are not all ignorant of the same things". This principle should guide team management. Each person has unique skills and knowledge that can contribute to the success of the company, provided they have a positive attitude and are willing to work as part of a team. An entrepreneur must create an environment where continuous learning is valued and where collaboration is encouraged over internal competition.

A company's true strength lies in its ability to function as a cohesive team. A team where each member understands his or her role, values the work of others and strives to achieve common goals is one of the greatest competitive advantages a company can have. This is only possible if leadership is able to recognise and leverage the individual strengths of each member, while working to improve weaknesses.

The Employer-Employee Relationship: A Necessary Alliance

It is important for politicians and legislators to understand that labour relations cannot be forced through regulations that discourage productivity or create an environment of distrust between employers and workers. Rather than imposing laws that seek to keep workers in their jobs at all costs, an environment should be fostered in which both employer and worker feel that they are in a mutually beneficial relationship.

Businesses must be seen for what they really are: living organisms that require the cooperation and contribution of all members to thrive. By fostering an environment in which employees feel valued and see their efforts recognised and rewarded, the company will not only survive, but thrive.

This symbiotic relationship between employers and employees is essential for long-term success. An employer must understand that the well-being of his or her employees is not only a matter of ethics, but also a matter of business strategy. Happy and motivated employees are more productive, more loyal and more creative, which ultimately translates into better results for the company.

Psychological Resilience: Key to Innovation and Growth

Resilience is the ability to adapt and recover quickly from adversity. In the business world, this quality is essential, as the environment is constantly changing and challenges can arise unexpectedly. A resilient entrepreneur not only survives crises, but also finds opportunities to innovate and grow.

The ability to remain flexible, to adjust strategies and to learn from failures is what enables companies not only to stay afloat, but to thrive in an increasingly competitive world. Resilience is not only a matter of internal strength, but also of being willing to continuously learn and evolve.

The Importance of Self-Care

Business success should not be achieved at the expense of the entrepreneur's mental and physical health. It is essential that business leaders understand the importance of self-care. Prolonged stress, burnout and lack of work-life balance can lead to the collapse not only of the individual, but also of the business.

Practising self-care means taking time to rest, reflect and recharge. This is not a sign of weakness, but of wisdom. An entrepreneur who takes care of him/herself is better equipped to lead his/her business to long-term success. Moreover, by modelling self-care, employers can foster a company culture that values wellbeing, which in turn can improve employee satisfaction and productivity.

Psychology as a Key to Business Success

Psychology is the foundation on which entrepreneurial success is built. An entrepreneur must be able to remain strong and resilient, face difficulties with determination and lead with empathy. But he or she must also be able to create an environment where his or her team can flourish, where talent is valued and where all members of the organisation work towards a common goal.

At the end of the day, success is not just measured in financial terms. It is measured in the ability to overcome challenges, the quality of the relationships we build and the positive impact we leave on the world. And to achieve all of this, psychological strength is arguably the most powerful tool an entrepreneur can have in his or her arsenal.

CHAPTER 13

SUCCESS STRATEGIES: WHAT THE GREAT ONES DO DIFFERENTLY

CHAPTER 13

SUCCESS STRATEGIES: WHAT THE GREAT ONES DO DIFFERENTLY

How are large companies structured?

Most businesses fail in their first five years of life and, in most cases, it is said that maybe the product didn't work, the service was at fault, the team was not good, the customer service failed, the entrepreneur was not good enough, or the productivity of the team was too low. But what if most of the reasons why all these companies fail are linked to their financial structure?

A large number of companies and self-employed in this country, and in many others, finance their capital needs through bank loans that must be repaid within an extremely short initial period (between 5 and 10 years). This timeframe is technically unfeasible at the outset, when all capital investment is directed towards building equity that is mostly created with resources that are tied up for the long term and that pay off in the same time span.

Herein lies one of the great paradoxes of modern entrepreneurship: how is it possible that so many entrepreneurs opt for a financial strategy that is so misaligned with the real needs of their business? The answer to this question could lie in the lack of adequate information or in the pressure exerted by financial institutions for entrepreneurs to take out loans that, in many cases, are not adequate for the sustainable development of their businesses.

I always carry out the same reasoning: do banks finance their economic activity with short-term or long-term economic resources? The answer is clear: always long-term. Banks are just another large company and, like most of them, they are financed through long-term immobilised economic resources, such as shares. No large company makes the mistake of financing its needs exclusively with short-term loans.

This is where many start-up entrepreneurs fall into a dangerous trap. The financial ratio of failing businesses is often set at a 90/10 ratio, i.e. 90% loan finance and only 10% partner or shareholder equity. However, the right balance is just the opposite ratio: 10% in loans and 90% in equity or investor capital.

By following this strategy, our company will have the competitive advantage of permanently tying up financial resources, successfully overcoming the cash flow disruptions that are common in most businesses. This not only provides stability, but also allows the company to focus its efforts on long-term growth without the burden of repaying large sums in short periods of time.

A Practical Example: Financing a Clothing Store

To analyse this strategy in more detail, let's take the example of an entrepreneur who decides to open a clothing shop and is confronted with the following financial data:

- **Security deposit for the premises:** 18.000€.
- **Refurbishment of premises:** 70.000€.
- **Initial stock:** 80.000€.
- **Total investment:** €168,000

Let us also assume the following monthly cost estimates:

- **Payroll costs:** 4.000€.
- **Rent:** 4.000€.
- **Supplies:** 250€.
- **Insurance:** €100
- **Total monthly costs:** €8,350

It is important to note that these costs do not include the monthly overheads for management overheads, consultancy, risk prevention, taxes, etc., which should be allocated proportionally to the number of sales units (shops) owned by the company.

Finally, let us consider this monthly income estimate:

- **Gross income:** €25,000
- **Revenue excluding VAT (21%):** 20.661€.
- **Revenue excluding manufacturing/acquisition cost (40%):** 12.396€.
- **Total net income:** 12.396€.

Outcome Option 1 (Investor/Shareholder Finance)

Let's assume that the initial investment needs (€168,000) have been financed through investors, shareholders or partners. This means that the capital does not have to be repaid in the short term, and there are no additional costs in the form of interest that put pressure on the company's finances from the outset.

Result: Income - Expenses: 12.396€ - 8.350€ = 4.046€. Annual return: 48.552€.

Assuming we have granted a 30% stake to our investors or shareholders:

- **Gross result for the investor:** €48,552 * 30% = €14,565.6.
- **Gross return on your investment:** €14,565.6 / €168,000 = 8.67%.
- **Total payback period:** 11.5 years.

From the strategic analysis of the company:

- **Total gross annual return after distribution of dividends to our investors or shareholders:** €48,552 - €14,565.6 = €33,986.4.
- **Annual return on sales:** €33,986.4 / (20,661 * 12) = 13.70%.
- **Current value of our company (with only one point of sale):** €606,900. This value is calculated using a multiple of 12.5, which is common for an estimated average annual return of 8% per investor.

This scenario shows how, by financing itself through investor or shareholder capital, the company is not only able to operate with stability, but is also positioned for sustained growth. The lack of pressure to repay large amounts of money in a short period of time allows the company to concentrate on expanding its operations, improving its products and services, and generating higher profits in the long run.

Result Option 2 (Bank Loan Financing)

Now, let us consider a scenario where the entire initial investment has been financed through a bank loan. Let us apply the following terms to the loan:

- **Amount:** 168.000€.
- **Interest rate:** 8%.
- **Term:** 4 years.
- **Monthly fee:** 4.101,37€.

The result would be:

Annual return: 48.552€ - (4.101,37€ * 12) = -664,44€.

BANKRUPT COMPANY.

That's right, the same company that is profitable in Option 1 is bankrupt in Option 2, even though all the data are exactly the same. Herein lies the very important difference that a large majority of entrepreneurs are unaware of, and which is the main reason why their businesses fail or do not grow beyond their potential.

This situation often occurs in different contexts: it may be due to lack of knowledge, because the entrepreneur is unwilling to share his or her business with others, or because the banking opportunities in their country do not offer an alternative financing option based on equity investment. In other words, banks only focus on financing most companies through bank loans and not on equity investment.

Why does this happen? There may be many reasons: banks may not be interested in taking shared risks, or they may be more interested in eventually failing these companies so that they can enforce as many liens as possible on all the equity they have built up over the years. Another reason could be that banks seek to keep control of the money in order to continue to control the future of the companies, or perhaps it is the only way they know how to maintain their results and equity on a permanent basis.

What is clear is one very important fact: if most banks are businesses and, as businesses, are financed primarily through the fixed capital permanently at their disposal, through their shareholders or through the money they keep at their disposal from their customers' accounts, why don't they advise or provide their entrepreneurial customers with the same financing system they use to be viable and successful businesses? Whatever the reason, one thing is clear: the more people we make information about this strategy available to, the more people will be able to successfully build successful businesses. In doing so, we will achieve a fairer distribution of income and contribute to a better future for our current and future societies.

Reflection on Financial Strategy

It is essential to reflect on this example, where the same company in Option 1 is a successful company and in Option 2 it is a bankrupt company. Option 2 is often the easiest option for starting a business because it involves approaching banks, presenting a project, and receiving financing based on borrowing capacity. However, this apparent ease is a trap that can lead to failure.

It is curious how, when we go to ask for money, banks ask us to demonstrate that we already have money, a secure source of income, and assets that can be easily seized in case of bankruptcy. Although some entrepreneurs believe that the solution is to create a limited company to limit liabilities, in many cases banks will require the entrepreneur to personally assume responsibility for the financing approved for his company.

It is not about avoiding responsibility for financing, but about making informed decisions about the financial structure of the company. Sometimes, the path that seems the easiest and quickest is the one that leads to the precipice. Option 1, although more difficult and slower, is the one that leads to building a large and successful enterprise. It requires overcoming many of the psychological limitations we have grown up with, and becoming a confident person in good times and bad. Keeping calm in a peaceful environment has no merit; keeping calm in a storm is what determines how prepared we are and how capable we are.

Overcoming Psychological and Cultural Barriers to Success

When we think of inviting people to be part of our project, what are the feelings that arise in our mind? Do we feel that we are offering others the opportunity to be part of a great project that will allow them to build a great heritage? Or do we feel that we are asking for money as if it were a handout? This mental constraint is one of the main limitations that the banks that control the money benefit from.

Our educational system, in many cases, hinders us when it comes to forming work teams. From school and university, we are encouraged to work individually, we are discouraged from creating synergies and sharing to achieve a great joint result. We are not taught to collaborate or to unite to achieve a common goal. Instead, we are taught to compete individually. How can we create great projects under this mentality?

A great entrepreneur must overcome this limitation. He must be able to. invite others to be part of his project, understanding that sharing is not losing, but multiplying the opportunities for success. He must be prepared to face both triumphs and failures, because the road to success involves experiencing both.

A few days ago, while signing a document in a notary's office, I overheard the conversation of an officer, Juan, who was worried because he had decided to rescind a sales contract that would mean losing several thousand euros. He could not sleep, saddened by the failure. I reminded him that he should not worry so much and that he should focus on his health, because failures are only part of the way. Without health, everything else becomes meaningless.

Problems are often simply issues that can be solved. Withdrawing your put option today may seem like a waste of money, but it could turn out to be an opportunity to make a bigger profit in the future. It is not the fall that is important, but the energy with which you pick yourself up after you have stumbled. In life, it is not the things that happen to us that matter, but the way we interpret them. Will I let this sink me or use it to make me stronger?

You have the answer, the decision is yours. Choose the right path.

Back to what we were discussing earlier....

Our education system is damaging us in this respect and in many others. Just yesterday, I was talking to my friends Martina and Miranda, aged 10 and 8 respectively, who told me that they had been forced to stop producing and selling bracelets. The reason? A teacher at school had accused them of being responsible for encouraging their classmates to "steal" coins from their mothers' and fathers' purses to buy the precious bracelets that they made with love, effort and dedication.

When I asked them how what they were telling me could be true and what their response to the teacher had been, they surprised me with their wit and common sense. They fearlessly argued that if one applied the same logic that the teacher had imposed on them, then one would also have to consider that these children were "stealing" coins to buy sweets, which are easily accessible but mostly considered junk food. This situation only reflects a profound truth about human nature and education. As the physicist Albert Einstein said: "There are only two infinite things, the universe and human stupidity, and I am not so sure about the former.

We can no longer allow our educational system to mislead future generations. We should not instill such profound misinformation about the monetary system in our children. We must take financial education in schools much more seriously, as it is one of the foundations that will prepare future generations for either success or failure. Misguiding them with poorly focused education from an early age is far more detrimental than we realize.

Shareholding

When building our own company, we will always encounter people who are reluctant to form a company composed of a large number of people. There is a common misconception that we will get better results if we keep the majority stake in our company, if we do not invite anyone to join our company, if we never share more than 51% of our company. However, let me make it clear that this is another major mistake that is made.

If you want to build a great project, you need a great team. No successful entrepreneur wants his or her company to get smaller every day; on the contrary, he or she wants it to grow, to generate higher profits, to employ more people, to increase its added value and to bring significant value to society.

The same is true for the number of shareholders: the greater the number of people in the company, the greater the wealth-building capabilities, the greater the resources with which you can create a great asset, and the greater the investment opportunities your company can pursue.

The belief that keeping 51% of your company in order not to lose control is a mistake. There are numerous cases of great entrepreneurs who diluted their shareholding well above that percentage and achieved considerable success. Let's look at a concrete example.

Scalability

As I mentioned earlier, I have on many occasions discussed with advisors, accountants and managers the strategy of sharing our partnerships with other people in order to build a great company, such as the one in Option 1. I remember one particular occasion when I was asked: "Would you invite a stranger into your home? However, we cannot limit our analysis to that interpretation. If we were to apply that logic to other situations, we could ask ourselves whether we would sleep on the mattresses in a hotel where thousands of people sleep, or whether we would eat on the plates, cutlery and glasses used in a restaurant. And the answer is yes, of course. We all do it every day when we use services in hotels and restaurants.

So the answer to the initial question is yes: of course I would invite a stranger to be part of my project. With the same security standards that we apply to other goods and services we share, it is possible to do so in a safe environment.

The right question we should all ask ourselves is: Would you rather be part of a project in which you own 100% of the company, but whose results are minimal or nil? Or would you rather be part of a company in which you only own 0.56%, equivalent to 8.34 million shares, valued at more than 630 million euros, and with an annual dividend distribution of more than 10 million euros? That is, to be part of a company that achieves annual sales of more than 47 billion euros, with an annual profit of more than 6 billion euros, equivalent to a 13.09% return on sales, with more than 1,000 of its own shops located in 170 countries. That company is called Nike, and its shareholder and main creator is Phil Knight.

As I said before, it is essential to have a secure structure that allows us to continue to lead our company towards the achievement of our objectives, maintaining the same spirit and values with which we created it on the first day. What do I mean by this? That the entrepreneur must continue to lead the company until he/she can delegate this responsibility to a person who possesses the same values and skills required for the position.

It is crucial to always have the right corporate structure that allows you to create a company that is characterised by ordinary shares and preference shares. Although the terminology may vary depending on the country in which you locate your company, the distinction between the two is clear: voting shares and non-voting shares. Both have different limitations and advantages, but both provide benefits to their holders. Voting shares will allow you to maintain control of the company, while non-voting shares, although they do not allow these new shareholders to control the company, will in most cases have a series of preferences, including preference in the distribution of dividends.

This way, even if you have shared 99.44% of your company, if with 0.56% you own the majority of the voting shares, you will still be able to run the company properly. How is this possible, you may be asking yourself? Imagine that 99% of the shares are non-voting and only 1% have voting rights. In other words, if you own 0.56% of that 1%, you have the majority of the shares with control in every decision making and, therefore, the direction of the company will remain yours.

Without complicating the explanation too much, as the more you research the more you will discover the wide range of different types of shares that can be issued, always focus on differentiating the percentage of total shares that are issued with voting and non-voting rights for each new issue of capital, so that you never lose sight of the total amount and percentage that you retain of both.

If in the country where you are currently located there are no facilities for setting up a structured company with shares offering this structure, you can always consider the option of moving, or even not having to move, as it is now possible to set up companies in many countries without the need to relocate. However, always pay attention to the company structure offered by that country and the tax regime that applies to it, as you will be competing globally and the more profit your company makes, the more competitive the price of the good or service you offer will be.

Finally, I invite you to conduct a thoughtful and detailed analysis using paper and pencil. Multiply the results of Option 1 by a strategy similar to the one we have discussed above and you can even incorporate the increase in the result if you add the savings from the monthly lease cost through the investment in the acquisition of premises, as was the case with McDonald's.

The strategy that McDonald's implemented, under the vision of co-founder Ray Kroc, is a shining example of how the acquisition of real estate assets can transform a business. Initially, McDonald's focused on expanding its restaurant chain through the franchise model. However, Kroc recognised that, to ensure a more stable and lasting revenue stream, it was essential not only to operate the restaurants, but also to own the land on which they were built.

By acquiring the land and buildings where its franchises were located, McDonald's not only secured considerable savings on lease costs, but also consolidated its financial and strategic power. This strategy made McDonald's one of the largest real estate companies in the world, generating revenue not only through the sale of hamburgers, but also by charging rents to its franchisees. This approach allowed the company to earn stable and recurring revenues, regardless of market fluctuations in food sales.

In addition, by controlling the properties, McDonald's was able to maintain strong leverage over its franchisees, ensuring that operational and brand standards were maintained at all times. This strategy not only reduced the risks associated with leasing, but also allowed the company to benefit from the appreciation in the value of its real estate assets over time.

In terms of performance, this strategy was instrumental in making McDonald's the global behemoth it is today. The acquisition of real estate has contributed significantly to the company's current valuation of over $200 billion. The income generated by its properties has provided McDonald's with a solid financial base that has allowed it to reinvest in its global expansion, innovate its products and maintain its position as a leader in the fast food industry.

Imagine a company that, instead of settling for a single outlet, similarly expands its presence by opening thousands of shops, each generating similar results to those we have analysed. Evaluate for yourself which of these strategies you consider most effective and advantageous in the long run.

I encourage you to not only assess this situation in the abstract, but also to take a close look at real, successful cases of great companies like Tesla, which has revolutionised the automotive industry, and innovative startups like Spotify, which has transformed the way we consume music. Both companies have adopted business models that prioritise a sound and visionary financial structure, where the need for capital to build an empire was prioritised, even if positive results took years to materialise.

In the case of Tesla, the company was founded in 2003 and did not reach profitability until 2020, after 17 years of continuous investment in research, development and expansion. Today, Tesla is valued at approximately $750 billion, a figure that reflects its impact on the industry and its leadership position in the transition to sustainable energy. By 2024, Tesla's net profit estimates stand at approximately $12.6 billion, a reflection of the long-term success of its business model.

Meanwhile, Spotify, founded in 2006, only managed to post a profit in 2019, after 13 years of operating at a loss while building a global music streaming platform. Today, Spotify has a valuation of approximately $30 billion, cementing its position as a leader in the streaming music market. As for projections for 2024, Spotify is expected to generate profits of around $1.2 billion.

These examples demonstrate that, by adopting an innovative and long-term financial structure, it is possible to build a solid and lasting empire. Tesla and Spotify, among others, are testament to the fact that patience, combined with a sound financial strategy, can lead to success even in an environment where rapid return expectations are the norm. So take a close look at the available data on the performance of these companies, and consider how you can apply these principles to your own projects.

It only took me 20 years to achieve overnight success.

"Peter O'Toole.

CHAPTER 14

INNOVATION AND ENTREPRENEURSHIP IN THE DIGITAL AGE

CHAPTER 14

INNOVATION AND ENTREPRENEURSHIP IN THE DIGITAL AGE

The digital era has radically transformed the way businesses are created, operate and grow. With the steady advance of technology, entrepreneurship is no longer a field limited to large investors or those with privileged access to resources. Today, anyone with an innovative idea and the determination to see it through can become a successful entrepreneur. This chapter explores how digitalisation and new technologies are democratising entrepreneurship, creating unprecedented opportunities and changing the business landscape forever.

1. The Digital Entrepreneurial Ecosystem: A New Era of Opportunity

The rise of the digital age has broken down many of the traditional barriers to entrepreneurship. Just a few decades ago, launching a business required considerable investment in infrastructure, staff and other physical resources. However, with the advent of the internet and digital platforms, entrepreneurs can now create and scale businesses from anywhere in the world with relatively low start-up capital and at breakneck speed.

A great and characteristic example that is generating enormous media coverage today is the ability of start-up companies such as OpenAI, which in just a few years since its founding in 2015 has managed to reach a market valuation of more than 90 billion dollars. This exponential growth contrasts with the historical trajectory of other major companies such as Nike, a company founded in 1964, which took decades to reach a similar stock market value.

The digital entrepreneurial ecosystem is characterised by its accessibility and the diversity of opportunities it offers. From e-commerce and digital marketing to mobile apps and software development, the possibilities are virtually limitless. In addition, global connectivity has enabled entrepreneurs to access international markets without the need for a physical presence, which has greatly expanded the reach and growth potential of their businesses.

Crowdfunding platforms have emerged as one of the most revolutionary tools in this ecosystem. Previously, project funding was limited to banks and institutional investors, which made it difficult for many brilliant ideas to see the light of day. Today, through platforms such as Crowdcube, FellowFunders, Seedrs, Kickstarter, Indiegogo and GoFundMe, entrepreneurs can present their projects directly to the public and obtain the necessary funds to carry them out. This democratisation of access to capital has allowed thousands of innovative projects to become a reality, without the need to access the only type of financing traditionally offered by banks.

Similarly, these platforms also represent an excellent opportunity for individual investors looking to get involved in startups and projects with high growth potential. Unlike stock market investing, where most listed companies have a limited growth path, crowdfunding allows investors to participate in early stage start-ups that, if successful, can generate significant returns. This ability to diversify and select projects with strong disruptive potential is a key advantage of crowdfunding, which is transforming not only how companies are funded, but also how they are built and grow.

2. Digital Business Models: Innovation in Value Creation

In the digital age, traditional business models have been challenged and, in many cases, replaced by more innovative and flexible models. One of the most prominent is e-commerce, which has revolutionised the way we buy and sell products. Companies such as Amazon and Alibaba have shown that, with the right strategy, an online business can outperform traditional retailers in terms of reach, convenience and profitability.

Another emerging model is SaaS (Software as a Service), which allows businesses and consumers to access software and digital services through subscriptions rather than one-off purchase licences. This model has been adopted by technology giants such as Microsoft and Adobe, and has proven to be highly cost-effective and scalable.

In addition, digital content and subscription platforms have enabled individual creators to monetise their knowledge and skills. From online courses, to social media posts, to paid podcasts and newsletters, digital entrepreneurs can generate recurring revenue while offering ongoing value to their audiences.

These digital business models have not only changed the way companies generate revenue, but have also created new ways of interacting with customers. Digital marketing, personalisation and automation enable companies to deliver highly personalised and engaging experiences, which in turn improves customer retention and increases customer lifetime value.

3. Digital Marketing and Growth: Strategies for Success

In a world where competition is fierce and consumers have more choice than ever before, digital marketing has become an indispensable tool for business success. Unlike traditional marketing, which is often costly and difficult to measure, digital marketing offers an effective and accessible way to reach a global audience.

One of the most effective strategies is SEO (Search Engine Optimisation), which allows businesses to improve their visibility on search engines and drive organic traffic to their websites. Through the creation of relevant content and technical optimisation, entrepreneurs can position themselves as leaders in their industry and attract potential customers on a consistent basis.

Social media also plays a crucial role in digital marketing strategy. Platforms such as Instagram, Facebook, LinkedIn and TikTok allow companies to build communities around their brands, interact directly with their customers and promote products and services in creative and targeted ways. Influencer marketing, in particular, has proven to be a powerful way to leverage the trust and credibility these individuals have with their followers.

Content marketing is another key strategy, involving the creation and distribution of valuable and relevant content to attract and retain a clearly defined audience. Whether through blogs, videos, podcasts or infographics, content marketing helps to build brand authority and educate potential customers, making it easier to convert them into loyal customers.

Finally, data analytics has become an indispensable tool for digital growth. By monitoring and analysing performance data, entrepreneurs can make informed decisions, optimise their marketing campaigns and improve the customer experience. Tools such as Google Analytics and CRM (Customer Relationship Management) allow businesses to track user behaviour, identify trends and adjust their strategies in real time to maximise results.

4. Success Stories and Lessons Learned

The digital age has spawned countless success stories that serve as inspiration for entrepreneurs around the world. Companies like Airbnb, Uber and Netflix started as small startups with disruptive ideas, and today they are global giants that have redefined entire industries.

Airbnb, for example, revolutionised the hotel industry by creating a platform that allows people to rent out their homes to travellers. What began in 2008 as a solution to pay for a flat rental in San Francisco has grown into a company valued at approximately $84 billion, with a presence in more than 190 countries. The key to its success was its ability to leverage digital technology and build a global community around its platform. Since its IPO in 2020, Airbnb has continued to expand, demonstrating the power of innovation in the digital age.

Uber, meanwhile, transformed the transportation industry by introducing a mobile app-based business model in 2009 that connects drivers with passengers. Its success, with a market capitalisation value of around $80 billion, is due to its focus on user convenience, cost optimisation and rapid global expansion. Since its IPO in 2019, Uber has continued to diversify its services to maintain its position in a competitive market.

Netflix is another emblematic example. Founded in 1997, it began as a DVD rental service by mail, and pioneered video streaming, an innovation that has transformed the way we consume entertainment. Today, with a market capitalisation of approximately $170 billion, its success lies in its ability to anticipate market trends and pivot its business model accordingly, investing in the creation of original content and using data to personalise the user experience. With hits such as House of Cards, Netflix has redefined the concept of global entertainment.

Several key lessons can be drawn from these success stories. First, constant innovation is essential in the digital age. Successful companies are those that are not afraid to reinvent themselves and adopt new technologies to stay relevant. Second, scalability is a crucial factor; digital business models, such as Airbnb, Uber and Netflix, are designed to grow exponentially with relatively low investment in physical resources, allowing them to expand globally quickly.

Ultimately, customer experience must be at the heart of any business strategy. Companies like Netflix have shown that understanding and anticipating user needs is vital to maintaining customer loyalty and continuing to grow. Using data and technology, they have been able to personalise product and service offerings, creating a unique experience that not only attracts but also retains customers.

In addition, it is essential to stress the importance of having a long-term vision. These companies focused not only on making immediate profits, but on building a solid foundation that would allow them to dominate the market in the long term. Investing in emerging technologies and maintaining a culture of internal innovation has been key to their sustained success.

These examples underline the relevance of globalisation. By expanding internationally, these companies have been able to tap into growing markets, diversify their revenues and reduce risks. In an increasingly connected world, the ability to adapt to different cultures and markets has become a crucial element for any company aspiring to global success.

5. The Future of Entrepreneurship: Emerging Trends

As technology continues to advance, so do the opportunities for digital entrepreneurship. Some of the emerging trends that promise to transform the business landscape in the coming years include artificial intelligence, blockchain, and virtual and augmented reality.

Artificial intelligence (AI) is beginning to be integrated into everything from customer service to product personalisation. Entrepreneurs who can leverage AI to automate processes, improve customer experience and make data-driven decisions will be in an advantageous position in the market.

The blockchain, beyond cryptocurrencies, offers opportunities for smart contract creation, supply chain management and transaction transparency. Entrepreneurs who understand and apply this technology will be able to innovate in sectors such as finance, logistics and intellectual property.

Virtual reality (VR) and augmented reality (AR) are opening up new possibilities for education, entertainment and commerce. As these technologies become more accessible, entrepreneurs have the opportunity to create immersive experiences that engage consumers in entirely new ways.

In addition, the gig economy continues to grow, allowing entrepreneurs to access a flexible, global workforce.

Platforms such as Fiverr, Upwork and Freelancer are making it easier for entrepreneurs and freelancers to connect, reducing operational costs and increasing business agility.

6. Innovation and Adaptation as Keys to Success

In short, the digital era has opened up an unprecedented range of opportunities for entrepreneurs. However, success in this environment requires more than a good idea; it requires a deep understanding of emerging trends, the ability to scale efficiently and a focus on customer experience.

Entrepreneurs who are able to stay at the forefront of technological innovation and adapt to changing market demands will be better positioned to thrive in the competitive digital world. This is an exciting time for entrepreneurship, full of possibilities and challenges that, with the right strategy, can be overcome to achieve lasting success.

Emerging capital raising platforms and new methods of accessing investors have added an extra dimension to this digital transformation, opening doors that were previously closed to many entrepreneurs and small investors. These tools have not only democratised access to capital, but have also changed the way projects are funded and eligible companies are created.

New Ways to Access Investors

Even beyond crowdfunding, new ways of connecting entrepreneurs with investors are also emerging. Platforms such as AngelList and StartEngine allow entrepreneurs to access networks of angel investors and venture capitalists who are interested in funding startups with high growth potential. These platforms combine the accessibility of crowdfunding with the strength of venture capital, offering entrepreneurs a viable alternative to traditional funding routes.

Equity crowdfunding has been central to the success of many recent startups, such as Wise (formerly TransferWise), which has revolutionised international money transfers. Wise, valued at approximately $11 billion, has used equity crowdfunding to raise capital and expand its user base rapidly. Similarly, companies such as Revolut and BrewDog have leveraged this strategy, reaching values of $33 billion and $2 billion, respectively. This type of financing not only democratises access to ownership, but also aligns the interests of entrepreneurs and investors, ensuring that both benefit from the company's success. These success stories demonstrate how equity crowdfunding can be a powerful tool to fuel the growth of start-ups with great market potential.

Another new trend emerging in the startup world is Media Equity, a model that also allows companies to exchange shares for advertising space in the media. This offers startups an innovative way to finance their marketing campaigns without spending cash, allowing them to achieve greater visibility and attract customers at an early stage. Media Equity aligns the interests of media and startups, as both benefit from the growth and success of the company. This strategy has great potential to amplify the results of marketing plans, especially in sectors where media presence is key to success.

The Global Impact of These Tools

The impact of these platforms and funding methods is global. They have enabled entrepreneurs around the world, including those in emerging economies, to access capital and resources that were previously out of reach. This expansion of access to capital has spurred innovation in a variety of industries and has allowed disruptive ideas to materialise without the constraints imposed by traditional funding methods.

For investors, these platforms offer a unique opportunity to diversify their portfolios beyond traditional stock market and real estate investments. By being able to invest in early stage startups and innovative projects, investors can participate in the growth of new companies that could become tomorrow's giants. This not only offers the potential for significant financial returns, but also allows them to be part of something bigger: the global drive for innovation and change.

New Risks and Considerations

However, with these new opportunities also come new risks. Projects funded through crowdfunding or startup investment platforms are often at very early stages, which carries a higher risk of failure. To minimise these risks, it is essential that you consolidate a solid and adequate financial education. This involves not only understanding the basics, but also deepening your analysis of the team behind each company, their strategies, and the market context in which they operate. Conducting thorough due diligence is not only advisable, but crucial to making informed investment decisions. With the right knowledge, investors can more accurately identify growth opportunities and minimise the risks inherent in these investments.

Transparency and clear communication are essential to ensure that every decision is backed by rigorous data and analysis. Thus, with proper preparation and a proactive attitude, it is possible to maximise the chances of success and participate positively and confidently in this exciting investment environment. In addition, the possibilities are invaluable, whether you are positioning yourself as an entrepreneur launching your project, or choosing to be an investor in successful new projects.

CHAPTER 15

THE FUTURE IS HERE: CRYPTOCURRENCIES, IA, METAVERSE AND THE TECH REVOLUTION

CHAPTER 15

THE FUTURE IS HERE: CRYPTOCURRENCIES, IA, METAVERSE AND THE TECH REVOLUTION

The future that we have so often seen anticipated in science fiction films is already here. These futuristic visions, which once seemed distant, are now part of our everyday reality. Despite the many efforts of some politicians to resist this change, technological evolution continues to advance unstoppably, and those who try to swim against this current inevitably drown, as we do when we try to swim against a storm at sea.

Cryptocurrencies: The Financial Revolution

Cryptocurrencies have emerged as a direct response to the irresponsible management of money by governments and central banks. For years, the uncontrolled printing of money, with no tangible basis between goods and services, has eroded citizens' purchasing power. Cryptocurrencies, with Bitcoin at the forefront, offer a decentralised alternative that seeks to combat this monetary devaluation. Being based on blockchain technology, they provide transparency, security and, most importantly, independence from traditional monetary policies.

The rise of cryptocurrencies has generated both enthusiasm and scepticism. On the one hand, they represent the possibility of a more equitable and manipulation-resistant financial system. On the other hand, their extreme volatility and the lack of a robust regulatory framework in many countries make them a high-risk option. However, this new financial paradigm cannot be ignored; it is an integral part of global economic evolution. As more institutions and governments explore the adoption of cryptocurrencies and blockchain technology, we are likely to see a radical transformation in the way we currently understand and use money.

Artificial Intelligence: The Transformation of the Labour Market

Artificial intelligence (AI) is already beginning to eliminate numerous jobs around the world. Systems capable of learning and adapting are replacing repetitive and predictable tasks, from manufacturing to customer service. This is not simply a technological advance; it is a profound transformation of the labour market that is altering the way people work and live.

AI is not only replacing jobs; it is also creating new ones. Technology industries are experiencing unprecedented growth, and with it, demand for skills related to programming, data analytics, and AI development. However, the speed of this transition poses a challenge: will today's workers be able to adapt quickly enough to stay relevant in this new landscape? This is a challenge both for individuals and for education and vocational training systems, which must evolve rapidly to prepare future generations.

In addition, AI is beginning to penetrate sectors that were once considered inherently human, such as creativity and decision-making. AI tools can now write, compose music, design products and even make medical diagnoses with an accuracy that rivals or surpasses humans. This evolution is redefining not only what jobs are needed, but also how the work itself is done. In the near future, it is likely that people will increasingly work in collaboration with AI systems, harnessing their capabilities to perform more complex and strategic tasks.

The Metaverse: The Next Digital Frontier and its Potential for Job Creation

In the vast and fast-paced landscape of technological innovation, a concept is emerging that promises to radically transform our interaction with the digital world: the Metaverse. Once the exclusive domain of science fiction, this term is rapidly coming to life thanks to advances in virtual reality, artificial intelligence and blockchain. The Metaverse is not just an extension of the internet as we know it; it is a new dimension where the physical and digital worlds intertwine in ways never before imagined.

The Metaverse represents a convergence of physical, augmented and virtual realities in a shared online space. Within this environment, users can work, socialise, shop, learn and even create digital assets that have value in the real world. This digital universe is driven by advanced technologies such as artificial intelligence, which personalises experiences, and blockchain, which ensures the ownership and authenticity of digital assets. As more people and businesses begin to explore and build in the

Metaverse, the economic opportunities expand exponentially.

One of the most promising aspects of the Metaverse is its potential for job creation. As this new digital ecosystem develops, countless opportunities arise for those willing to adapt and take advantage of its possibilities. Professionals in graphic design, programming, virtual experience development, digital architecture, and virtual community management will be essential to build and maintain this new world. In addition, the Metaverse will open doors to new forms of digital entrepreneurship, allowing individuals to create and monetise content, services and products within this virtual space.

The potential impact of the Metaverse is vast and multifaceted. Imagine a world where physical boundaries are irrelevant, where people can meet, work and play regardless of their geographic location. This new digital ecosystem could transform sectors such as commerce, education, health and entertainment, offering immersive experiences that were previously impossible. Businesses, for example, could set up virtual offices that enable real-time global collaboration, while consumers could try products in virtual shops before buying them in the real world.

For those who adapt to the new skill demands of the Metaverse, an unprecedented window of opportunity is opening up. Digital marketing professionals, virtual reality content developers, cybersecurity specialists and user experience consultants will see an increase in demand for their skills. Furthermore, the Metaverse economy could facilitate job creation for a younger, technologically literate generation, who will find in this environment a platform to innovate and thrive.

However, as with any disruptive innovation, the Metaverse also presents significant challenges. Privacy, security, intellectual property and regulation are areas that will need to be addressed to ensure that this new digital universe is inclusive, secure and sustainable. In addition, the development of the Metaverse requires a robust and accessible technological infrastructure, which raises questions about the digital divide and equitable access to these new technologies.

As the Metaverse continues to evolve, its impact on the global economy and our daily lives will be profound. Countries and companies that lead in the adoption and development of this new environment will have a significant competitive advantage in the economy of the future. The Metaverse is not just an extension of the internet; it is the next great frontier, one that is set to redefine the way we live, work and interact in the digital age. And for those willing to adapt and seize its opportunities, it represents a gateway to new forms of employment, creativity and economic prosperity.

Autonomous Transport Systems and the Future of Mobility

Autonomous transport systems are in full swing and are set to revolutionise the way we move and transport goods. From autonomous cars to delivery drones, these systems promise unprecedented efficiency, with lower operating costs and a significant reduction in human error. Countries and economies that embrace these technologies will lead the next era of global mobility.

The impact of this technology goes beyond simply replacing human drivers. Autonomous systems have the potential to drastically reduce traffic accidents, cut carbon emissions and optimise supply chains to previously unimaginable levels. Mass adoption of these systems could also transform cities, making transport more accessible, safe and efficient for all.

However, those who resist this change will face severe economic consequences. Industries that rely on human labour in transportation, such as truck drivers, taxis, and delivery services, will see a radical transformation. Countries that do not adapt their policies and economies to integrate these technologies will be left behind, facing unfair competition and possible economic bankruptcy as others adopt more efficient and cost-effective transport systems.

Robots and New Productive Capabilities

Automation is not limited to transport; robots are revolutionising industrial production in all sectors. These automated systems can operate 24/7, with operating costs limited mainly to the energy needed to keep them running. This contrasts with human labour, which requires wages, benefits and is limited by fatigue and the need for breaks.

Those companies and countries that succeed in combining automation with low-cost and renewable energy sources will have a significant competitive advantage. The ability to produce goods and services more efficiently and economically will be crucial in the future global economy. We are not simply talking about an evolution; we are witnessing a revolution that could surpass even the impact of the Industrial Revolution in its time.

This shift is also redefining the concept of work. As robots take on repetitive and dangerous tasks, humans have the opportunity to focus on more strategic, creative and relational roles. However, this transition will not be easy for everyone. Those who are not prepared to adapt to an increasingly automated work environment may find it difficult to remain competitive in the marketplace.

The Future That Is Already Present: Innovations Transforming Society

The future has already begun to manifest itself in our present. Tools like ChatGPT and other artificial intelligence-based systems are revolutionising entire fields. Content creators, graphic designers, programmers, and scientists are seeing their tasks become more productive and less costly thanks to these technologies. The automation of routine tasks is allowing professionals to focus on more creative and strategic aspects of their work.

These technologies are not only improving efficiency, they are also democratising access to advanced capabilities. A small business owner or individual entrepreneur now has access to tools that were previously only available to large corporations with huge budgets. This is levelling the playing field and allowing more people to compete and succeed in a global marketplace.

These changes, while beneficial in many respects, are also creating tensions in the labour market. The elimination of certain roles and the creation of new specialised jobs is creating a gap that can leave those who do not adapt quickly behind. It is a critical time when continuing education and adaptation are key to staying competitive in a rapidly changing world of work.

Economic Consequences and Changes in Consumption Habits

The economic crises that are affecting many countries, including Spain, Europe and the United States, are not simply the result of bad economic policies. They are symptoms of a deeper transition to a new digital and automated economy. Uncontrolled money printing during the pandemic, coupled with policies that encouraged stagnant economic activity, has led to runaway inflation and unsustainable public debt.

As consumption habits change, driven by technology and globalisation, economies that fail to adapt will see an inevitable decline. Governments that continue to spend without creating new and sustainable sources of revenue will be condemning their citizens to an ever-increasing fiscal burden. This cycle of unsustainable public borrowing and spending can lead to an economic crisis from which it will be difficult to recover.

It is crucial to understand that these changes in consumer habits are not temporary; they represent a structural shift in how people interact with the market. The rise of e-commerce, the preference for on-demand services, and the increasing importance of sustainability are reshaping economies at an accelerating pace. Countries and companies that do not adapt to these new realities will be at a disadvantage compared to those that are already innovating.

The Challenge of Adapting to Change

Employers do not want to lay off employees or downsize their operations. However, in a competitive global environment, adaptation is essential. Policies that attempt to block layoffs or penalise technological innovation will only delay the inevitable and make the transition more painful for everyone.

The more a society resists innovations that are already here, the deeper the negative impact on its economy. Societies that do not take control of their economies and do not generate bigger and better sources of income will continue to blame external factors rather than take responsibility for their own future.

The key to meeting these challenges lies in education and lifelong learning. It is essential that both workers and employers keep up to date with the latest trends and technological developments. Those who invest in employee training and innovation will have a greater chance of surviving and thriving in this new economic environment.

The Role of Automation and Individual Responsibility

Many workers are being confused or misinformed about the real impact of automation. Soon, many physical tasks will be performed by robots with greater efficiency and precision. From vegetable picking to transportation to customer service, robots are on their way to replacing human workers in many areas.

However, rather than fearing these changes, it is crucial that workers adapt and focus on developing skills that are harder to automate: creativity, innovation, and common sense. Seizing the opportunities offered by new technologies is the key to staying relevant and successful in the economy of the future.

Adaptation is not only necessary at the individual level, but also at the societal level. It is imperative that public policies encourage innovation, education and the development of advanced skills. Those countries that invest in educating their populations to integrate into this new automated environment will have a significant advantage in the global economy. Automation does not have to be an enemy; it can be an opportunity to free workers from repetitive tasks and allow them to focus on more satisfying, higher value-added jobs. Moreover, workers will no longer be limited to operating solely in the wage labour quadrant. Thanks to numerous innovations, they now have greater opportunities to become successful investors and entrepreneurs, accessing all new forms of financial and personal growth.

Final Reflection

I sincerely hope that this book has been a valuable tool in your journey towards a deeper and more practical understanding of personal and global economics. My intention has been not only to provide you with knowledge on how to improve your financial situation, but also to inspire you to approach life with a contribution-oriented and growth-oriented mindset. We live in a society where money often remains a taboo subject, a concept that many prefer not to mention because they mistakenly associate it with greed or corruption. However, this stigma is nothing more than a reflection of ignorance, a direct consequence of an education system that fails to teach us the real rules of money, even though it is one of the most essential life skills.

Money is a tool, neither good nor bad in itself, but powerful in the hands of those who understand how it works and know how to use it for good. It is crucial to understand that money is not only necessary to meet our basic needs, but also to achieve our highest aspirations and, most importantly, to contribute to the well-being of others. Hopefully, this book has helped you to demystify money, to see it not as an end in itself, but as a means to live a richer life, in every sense of the word.

I invite you to reflect on how the economic system works and how you can use that knowledge to build real assets - assets that generate income and wealth in a sustainable way. Don't just try to solve the income minus expenses equation by reducing expenses; instead, focus on increasing your income. This is the path that will allow you to live a fuller life, a life where you are not forced to sacrifice your dreams and goals for mere financial survival.

It is vital that you challenge yourself to step out of whatever comfort zone you find yourself in, because growth and true prosperity are never born out of comfort. Learning from mistakes is a fundamental part of the road to success. Every setback is not a failure, but a lesson, an opportunity to improve and strengthen yourself for future battles. Don't beat yourself up over failures; see them as the foundation on which you will build a stronger and more successful future.

Albert Einstein once said: "Insanity is doing the same thing over and over again and expecting different results". Don't fall into the trap of living life as a being who repeats the same actions every day expecting a change. Dare to take charge of your destiny, start your own business or join projects that present great investment opportunities.

The most important thing is not to let time run out, because it passes faster than we think. The sooner you decide to expand your field of investment, the more you increase your chances of success. Because as my grandfather once said to me in his 90s: "Nobody gets rich by being just a worker".

Finally, remember that life is a journey whose length we cannot control, but we can decide how we travel it. Make sure that instead of simply adding days to your life, you are adding life to your days. Live with purpose, with passion, and with the knowledge that every day you invest in your personal growth and in building your legacy is a day well lived.

Success is not a destination, but a continuous journey of learning, improvement and contribution. I wish you all the best on your journey!

THANK YOU TO THE READER:

I want to sincerely thank you for making it this far, for taking the time and energy to explore the ideas and strategies I have shared in this book. Purchasing this book is more than just a purchase; it is a commitment to yourself to learn, grow and transform your financial life. I hope that the knowledge you have gained will inspire you to take actions that will lead you to a more fulfilling and successful life, both personally and professionally.

Your decision to read and apply these concepts not only has the potential to improve your life, but also to positively influence those around you. In doing so, you become part of a movement that seeks real and lasting change - change that goes beyond economics to touch the most fundamental aspects of what it means to live a purposeful life.

Thank you for trusting me and this book as a guide on your path to a better future. I wish you every success on your journey, and remember that every step you take forward is a step towards realising your dreams.

> "THE TRUE SUCCESS LIES NOT IN HOW MUCH MONEY YOU ACCUMULATE, BUT IN THE POSITIVE IMPACT YOU LEAVE ON THE WORLD AND THE LIVES YOU TRANSFORM".
>
> - JORGE ZAGUIRRE VILLANUEVA -

This book is a reflection of my own personal and financial journey, written in the hope of inspiring you to look at money in a different way. It is not just a guide to improving your finances; it is an invitation to rediscover your purpose and to align your financial decisions with the values that truly matter in your life.

My hope is that, through these pages, you will find the motivation to use money as a tool to create a positive and lasting impact on your life, your legacy and the world.

JORGE ZAGUIRRE VILLANUEVA